FEARLESS

FAITH

Bravery, Courage & Confidence in a Changing World

MATTHEW ASHIMOLOWO

Printed 2020

© 2020 Matthew Ashimolowo

Published by Mattyson Media an imprint of MAMM Matthew Ashimolowo Media Ministries, Buckmore Park, Maidstone Road, Chatham, Kent ME5 9QG

www.pastormatthew.tv

ISBN: 978-1-909158-36-8

CONTACT MATTHEW ASHIMOLOWO

Twitter: @MatAshimolowo

Instagram: ma.ashimolowo

Facebook: Matthew A. Ashimolowo

Fearless Faith

Table of contents

Fearless Faith

The world is in crisis. Christianity is in crisis.

A world of almost eight billion people has been gripped by unprecedented fear: we cannot see the Coronavirus but we can see its effects as it takes lives.

Nations are in lockdown. The streets are deserted. Families are in despair because they do not know who will make it through this modern pandemic.

Neighbours are unable to show affection for fear of infection.

Beyond the challenge, Christianity is in crisis. There is an erosion of our faith by other religions. The biggest recipients of the consequences of religious terrors have been the Christians.

False religions have invaded Christian Europe. The Church is quiet in order to be politically correct. It is cowering in a corner, losing its members and selling away its buildings to the highest bidder.

In other parts of the world where Christianity still thrives e.g. Africa, middle and upper middle class Christians stay silent when the Church is bastardised and its vulnerable members brutalised.

Our response has been one of fear. We are afraid of persecution or possibly death.

Fear is a bad master. Fear has torment. It is a destroyer which acts faster than most other sources. Fear magnifies limitations and other challenges. It makes a big thing out of something small.

It is time for us to live by faith and not by sight. To do this, we need to raise a generation of bravehearts, conquerors, and champions and people of extreme confidence, people who will turn the tide.

The world is ripe for the generation of the fearless to rise.

This book is the igniting force to set you on fire for God and make you zealous, full of faith and able to walk in power and victory.

Fearless Faith

BRAVEHEART

Solomon declares that truly brave people are as bold as a lion.

You never see a lion surrounded by a group of bodyguards. Rather, the lion, though eight feet long and yet with a slim body, probably less than a meter wide will take on an elephant that is twenty times its size or a buffalo, which, by the swinging of its horns can gore a lion. However, the bravery of a lion, as captured in this verse, will make a lion attempt anything.

Bravehearts!

The best way to describe this kind of people is that they are daring, with courageous faith. They are unlikely heroes. They take bold stands. They are unusually audacious, dauntless in the face of what should make one afraid, defiant of what comes against them, fearless almost to a fault, gallant in war, possess a gutsy spirit to take on battles, indomitable by challenges, lion-hearted and unafraid.

This kind of spirit is captured in the story we see in 2 Samuel 23:8-39.

> "These are the names of the mighty men whom David had: Josheb-Basshebeth the Tachmonite, chief among the captains. He was called Adino the Eznite, because he had killed eight hundred men at one time. And after him was Eleazar the son of Dodo, the Ahohite, one of the three mighty men with David when they defied the Philistines who were gathered there for battle, and the men of Israel had retreated. He arose and attacked the Philistines until his hand was weary, and his hand stuck to the sword. The Lord brought about a great victory that day; and the people returned after him only to plunder. And after him was Shammah the son of Agee the Hararite. The Philistines had gathered together into a troop where there was a piece of ground full of lentils. So the people fled from the Philistines. But he stationed himself in the middle of the field, defended it, and killed the Philistines. So the Lord brought about a great victory. Then three of the thirty chief men went down at harvest time and came to David at the cave of Adullam. And the troop of

Philistines encamped in the Valley of Rephaim. David was then in the stronghold, and the garrison of the Philistines was then in Bethlehem. And David said with longing, "Oh, that someone would give me a drink of the water from the well of Bethlehem, which is by the gate!" So the three mighty men broke through the camp of the Philistines, drew water from the well of Bethlehem that was by the gate, and took it and brought it to David. Nevertheless he would not drink it, but poured it out to the Lord. And he said, "Far be it from me, O Lord, that I should do this! Is this not the blood of the men who went in jeopardy of their lives?" Therefore he would not drink it. These things were done by the three mighty men. Now Abishai the brother of Joab, the son of Zeruiah, was chief of another three. He lifted his spear against three hundred men, killed them, and won a name among these three. Was he not the most honored of three? Therefore he became their captain. However, he did not attain to the first three. Benaiah was the son of Jehoiada, the son of a valiant man from Kabzeel, who had done many deeds. He had killed two lion-like heroes of Moab. He also had gone down and killed a lion in the midst of a pit on a snowy day. And he killed an Egyptian, a spectacular man. The Egyptian had a spear in his hand; so he went down to him with a staff, wrested the spear out of the Egyptian's hand, and killed him with his own spear. These things Benaiah the son of Jehoiada did, and won a name among three mighty men. He was more honored than the thirty, but he *did not attain to the first three. And David appointed him over his guard. Asahel the brother of Joab was one of the thirty; Elhanan the son of Dodo of Bethlehem, Shammah the Harodite, Elika the Harodite, Helez the Paltite, Ira the son of Ikkesh the Tekoite, Abiezer the Anathothite, Mebunnai the Hushathite, Zalmon the Ahohite, Maharai the Netophathite, Heleb the son of Baanah (the Netophathite), Ittai the son of Ribai from Gibeah of the* children of Benjamin, Benaiah a

They are daring, with courageous faith!

Pirathonite, Hiddai from the brooks of Gaash, Abi-Albon the Arbathite, Azmaveth the Barhumite, Eliahba the Shaalbonite (of the sons of Jashen), Jonathan, Shammah the Hararite, Ahiam the son of Sharar the Hararite, Eliphelet the son of Ahasbai, the son of the Maachathite, Eliam the son of Ahithophel the Gilonite, Hezrai the Carmelite, Paarai the Arbite, Igal the son of Nathan of Zobah, Bani the Gadite, Zelek the Ammonite, Naharai the Beerothite (armorbearer of Joab the son of Zeruiah), Ira the Ithrite, Gareb the Ithrite, and Uriah the Hittite: thirty-seven in all." 2 Samuel 23:8-39

What a catalogue! It lists David's mighty warriors: mighty men, men who were fearless and yet, served God.

What shall be said of the first one listed?

"These are the names of the mighty men whom David

had: Josheb-Basshebeth the Tachmonite, chief among the captains. He was called Adino the Eznite, because he had killed eight hundred men at one time." 2 Samuel 23:8

He raised his spear against eight-hundred men and killed them in one encounter. This is almost unimaginable unless it is probably the kind of scene you see in a film, where the hero takes on a crowd of enemies and each person waits for their own turn to fight. I do not think that is the case here. This is a man with a dauntless, gutsy, indomitable, fearless faith.

Next to him was Eleazar, the son of Dodo. When there was no battle, 2 Samuel 23:9 says that he and his friends went and taunted the Philistines so they could come out to fight. When the Philistines came, Eleazar fought until his hand became stuck to his sword and the Lord brought about a great victory that day.

The whole of this chapter speaks of men who stand in a class of their own - beyond Superman, Spiderman, Ironman and all the fictional characters created by the entertainment world.

How did they become bravehearts? What was their secret? The secret of a braveheart is that it comes from the Lord.

Do we need this kind of heart today? Yes. Christianity is in crisis. Christianity is at a crossroads. I travel around the world and if you keep abreast of the stories of nations that used to be Christian, there is an eroding by other religions, by belief systems that were once standard. Christianity stands almost powerless, unable to make a change. Christians have joined the politically correct, being unable to speak out.

I have lived in the United Kingdom for thirty-five years as at the time of writing this book. When I look at how and what shift has happened, I feel a great sense of fear and shame because the Church has cowered into a corner and only tries to practically defend its little corner while false religion invades Europe. The fastest growing religions are the ones that have entered Europe during the last couple of years.

Churches are being sold. Christians are denying their faith. Church denominations are rewriting their beliefs. Synod meetings are being called to question the veracity of the doctrines previously held dear. Christians are now apologetic for the things they once believed in. This calls for brave hearts.

In certain parts of the world, in my original country, Nigeria, for example, while there is a wild growth of Christianity, which has led to the largest church building

Do we need this kind of heart today? Yes!

ever, the largest gathering of Christians ever, the largest worship experience ever only being found in the nation of Nigeria, yet, middle class Christians who have found themselves in places of power have been largely silent when fellow Christians in vulnerable places have been slaughtered or when there has been a penetration of other religions.

Believers who profess Christ, who have found themselves in places of authority and opportunity have been unable to express a fearless faith in the face of dogmas and doctrines that are demonic and promote the killing of anyone who does not adhere to what they believe.

We need brave hearts. Bravehearts' stand is a key to victory in warfare. It gives you victory and access to a new realm. A brave heart is the key to taking what the enemy stole. Jesus took the lid off when He told us that the thief only comes to take everything.

"The thief does not come except to steal, and to kill, and to destroy. I have come that they may have life, and that they may have it more abundantly." John 10:10

It is very easy to quote that verse, but we must realise it requires brave hearts to go into house of the strong man and dispossess him.

"No one can enter a strong man's house and plunder his goods, unless he first binds the strong man. And then he will plunder his house." Mark 3:27

Braveheart is boldness. Boldness comes from the Hebrew 'Phares.' This word is also the same word which describes breaking through, breaking forth, breaking in, breaking out.

Phares is to be outspoken. It is for words to come out of frankness. Phares is bluntness; however, what we see today is apologetic statements and heads of church bodies being afraid to make statements because they do not want their systems persecuted.

Phares is assurance. Phares is confidence. This kind of boldness is outspokenness. It is the grace which causes you to speak boldly and act confidently.

THE MANIFESTO OF BRAVEHEARTS

When I get to eternity, some of the people I would like to meet are the men in 2 Samuel 9. Men who singlehandedly took on battles that a whole company of people would have taken a flight from.

The manifesto of this kind of men is that:

1. Bravehearts refuse to be beaten by life

When life throws them a lemon, they turn it to lemonade. When life throws them a mess, they turn it to a message. When choices come, they make the choice which they know is consequential upon their chances.

2. Bravehearts know that kindness takes courage

3. Bravehearts believe in the impossible

How else would one man take on eight-hundred other people? It is a certain kind of bravery that makes a man not walk out into battle in bravado or foolish presumption but a certain confidence in God that He has never lost a battle.

4. Bravehearts see the end result, not the fight at hand

"To him who overcomes I will give to eat from the tree of life, which is in the midst of the Paradise of God." Revelation 2:7b

"To him who overcomes I will give some of the hidden manna to eat. And I will give him a white stone, and on the stone a new name written which no one knows except him who receives it." Revelation 2:17b

Bravehearts' stand is a key to victory in warfare

"And he who overcomes, and keeps My works until the end, to him I will give power over the nations. 'He shall rule them with a rod of iron; They shall be dashed to pieces like the potter's vessels' as I also have received from My Father; and I will give him the morning star." Revelation 2:26-28

"He who overcomes shall be clothed in white garments, and I will not blot out his name from the Book of Life; but I will confess his name before My Father and before His angels." Revelation 3:5

"He who overcomes, I will make him a pillar in the temple of My God, and he shall go out no more. I will write on him the name of My God and the name of the city of My God, the New Jerusalem, which comes down out of heaven from My God. And I will write on him My new name." Revelation 3:12

"To him who overcomes I will grant to sit with Me on My throne, as I also overcame and sat down with My Father on His throne." Revelation 3:21

5. Bravehearts fight like unstoppable people

But, interestingly enough, they find beauty in ragged and rugged places.

This is what motivates them:

⮑ the beauty of being crowned after victory,

⮑ the beauty of knowing that the battle belongs to the Lord,

⮑ the beauty of knowing that vengeance belongs to God,

⮑ the beauty of knowing that the fight is not in vain but to advance the Kingdom of God.

THE MAKING OF BRAVEHEARTS

You can only be a braveheart if you choose to be a mountain mover.

"For assuredly, I say to you, whoever says to this mountain, 'Be removed and be cast into the sea,' and does not doubt in his heart, but believes that those things he says will be done, he will have whatever he says. Therefore I say to you, whatever things you ask when you pray, believe that you receive them, and you will have them." Mark 11:23-24

There are those who would rather run away from the mountain, walk around the mountain, talk about the mountain, dance around the mountain or sit around the mountain.

"On this side of the Jordan in the land of Moab, Moses began to explain this law, saying, "The Lord our God spoke to us in Horeb, saying: 'You have dwelt long enough at this mountain." Deuteronomy 1:5-6

Bravehearts will move the mountain. If it will not move, they will tunnel through it. Bravehearts are water walkers. We see this with Peter, even though he expressed timidity later, for a brief moment he expressed this candid spirit of a braveheart, asking Jesus to bid him to walk on water.

"And Peter answered Him and said, "Lord, if it is You, command me to come to You on the water." So He said, "Come." And when Peter had come down out of the boat, he walked on the water to go to Jesus." Matthew 14:28-29

Bravehearts have another side to them. They chase after Jesus with a tender, world-changing wildness.

"Now after Jesus was born in Bethlehem of Judea in the days of Herod the king, behold, wise men from the East came to Jerusalem, saying, "Where is He who has been born King of the Jews? For we have seen His star in the East and have come to worship Him."" Matthew 2:1-2

"When they saw the star, they rejoiced with exceedingly great joy. And when they had come into the house, they saw the young Child with Mary His mother, and fell down and worshiped Him. And when they had opened their treasures, they presented gifts to Him: gold, frankincense, and myrrh." Matthew 2:10-11

We see bravehearts in the wise men who came from the Far East to look for Jesus. Imagine the number of mountainous terrains they had to cross. If by today's geography we assume that the world was similar to what it is now, then it means they went through the deserts of Arabia or the Sahara, all in pursuit of the One who came that we may find life.

It must have taken those bravehearts a journey of months to seek Him whose star they saw in the East.

"saying, "Where is He who has been born King of the Jews? For we have seen His star in the East and have come to worship Him."" Matthew 2:2

Did they fight battles? Did they meet with challenges? Like these wise men, bravehearts never give in. Bravehearts never give up. Bravehearts never let go.

It is not part of Christianity, when confronted with battles, to just announce, "Let us just leave everything to God." These are blanket statements that may have crept into Christianity from religions that taught fatalism. Christianity is not about fate, accepting life as it comes, but faith, believing God and trusting for change to happen.

Bravehearts will make the extraordinary look ordinary, as if it is just regular. Imagine the man who taunts an entire Philistine army and when they come, he fights until his hand is clasped to the sword. Imagine the one who took on two lion-like men in a snow pit and yet came out victorious. They make the extraordinary look ordinary.

I believe Paul was one of them. Through his pen and his voice, he expressed fearless faith.

"I can do all things through Christ who strengthens me."
Philippians 4:13

They fight like warriors and yet cry like children. Imagine David at the news of the death of Jonathan and Saul. He cried like a child. Though they are bravehearts, they are tender when it comes to the convictions of God.

Bravehearts will skin their knees and let them carry the scars that bear them witness that they have 'been there, done that and have the t-shirt'.

Bravehearts never give up

Bravehearts know that they are not ordinary and therefore cannot settle for ordinary. They must put the 'extra' before the ordinary.

They know they are called to be kings with a domain.

"Then God blessed them, and God said to them, "Be fruitful and multiply; fill the earth and subdue it; have dominion over the fish of the sea, over the birds of the air, and over every living thing that moves on the earth.""
Genesis 1:28

It is very easy to talk of dominion and make it a conference theme, but to walk the walk and talk the talk requires that a person to have a brave heart.

Bravehearts know they are called to be warriors. I cannot get over the man who taunted the enemy. True bravehearts are always looking for new mountains to climb for the Lord, new grounds to pick, taking territories, raising champions.

Bravehearts know they are called to be mentors because life has its time limits and yet Christianity must not be void of witnesses. They never do it alone. They raise tomorrow's champions.

Bravehearts know they are works of art, they are unique, here to make an impact. They know they are not a stereotype; they are unique.

"I will praise You, for I am fearfully and wonderfully made; Marvelous are Your works, and that my soul knows very well. My frame was not hidden from You, when I was made in secret, and skillfully wrought in the lowest parts of the earth. Your eyes saw my substance, being yet unformed. And in Your book they all were written, the days fashioned for me, when as yet there were none of them. How precious also are Your thoughts to me, O God! How great is the sum of them! If I should count them, they would be more in number than the sand; when I awake, I am still with You." Psalm 139:14-18

Bravehearts know that they are not mere role players or specks on a massive planet. They know they are world-shapers, decision-makers, decision-changers.

"I beseech you therefore, brethren, by the mercies of God, that you present your bodies a living sacrifice, holy, acceptable to God, which is your reasonable service. And do not be conformed to this world, but be transformed by

the renewing of your mind, that you may prove what is that good and acceptable and perfect will of God." Romans 12:1-2

They know they are not called to conform, they have been sent to transform.

Compare this truth with the world in which we find ourselves today. Christianity has moved goalposts and as a result we are afraid to speak against the things we see today. What we used to be proud of, we are now told to hide in our closets because it is considered 'archaic, Adamic or Victorian.'

Bravehearts are dream machines who birth tomorrow. They command tomorrow before it comes. They see five years before it manifests.

""Have you commanded the morning since your days began, and caused the dawn to know its place," Job 38:12

Bravehearts are unexpected warriors. They do not always look it on the outside but, give them tomorrow and they will deliver change.

Bravehearts have got secret agents of grace. In a world that is messed up, with millions of street children, a generation that has given itself up to prostitution and drug abuse, bravehearts go boldly where others dread and bring grace as a weapon that conquers the most difficult hearts.

> Be remembered for being around and making a great impact instead of being a victim in your own victim story

"For though I am free from all men, I have made myself a servant to all, that I might win the more; and to the Jews I became as a Jew, that I might win Jews; to those who are under the law, as under the law, that I might win those who are under the law; to those who are without law, as without law (not being without law toward God, but under law toward Christ), that I might win those who are without law; to the weak I became as weak, that I might win the weak. I have become all things to all men, that I might by all means save some."1 Corinthians 9:19-22

THE MANIFESTATION OF BRAVEHEARTS

Be the braveheart with gentle hands. Jesus said, "serve in my vineyard."

"And said to them, 'You also go into the vineyard, and whatever is right I will give you.' So they went." Matthew 20:4

Have you ever noticed that vineyards are a place where someone needs tender hands to take the harvest off the vines or else the grapes are crushed and the juice is lost?

Be a braveheart. Take the space where you find yourself. It could be the kitchen or the boardroom and yet, in those places, you can be the braveheart God called you to be.

Do not stay on the shelf. Do not retire mentally, physically, emotionally, spiritually and otherwise. Go all out.

Be remembered for being around and making a great impact instead of being a victim in your own victim story. Rather, be the victim who stepped out and changed everything.

Let the world study your conquest, not your inquest. Let it be said that when you were around, you changed things, you moved things, you shook things.

Make history, step out of the lines that are already drawn. It is very interesting to see how easy it is to confine oneself and conform to the lines already drawn. Stepping out of the box can actually be used as 'slang' unless you consciously call yourself to order and pull yourself out of the box that both you and others have created.

It is time to be a braveheart.

Shake the jar up. Never stop being in the 'becoming' zone.

"Beloved, now we are children of God; and it has not yet been revealed what we shall be, but we know that when He is revealed, we shall be like Him, for we shall see Him as He is." 1 John 3:2

However, be tender towards your own failures. Do not let them stop you. Do not let them hold you. One of the ways to do that is to never call a pity party. Never remind yourself of your failures, rather, remember your humanity but, beyond that, know that you are not divinity. You are just one son of God whom He has empowered to take on His world and through Him, you will not fail.

Make fear work for you when it shows.

"Fear not, for I am with you; be not dismayed, for I am your God. I will strengthen you, yes, I will help you, I will uphold you with My righteous right hand.'" Isaiah 41:10

As a human being who lives in this body and on this planet, once in a while you will need the things that make you dread. Rather, let the fear work for you.

Live the life you were created for. You were created to dominate, to subdue, to bless, to increase.

"Then God blessed them, and God said to them, "Be fruitful and multiply; fill the earth and subdue it; have dominion over the fish of the sea, over the birds of the air, and over every living thing that moves on the earth.""
Genesis 1:28

Show what you were made to offer your world. You came here fully loaded. Do not go back with the goods in you undelivered. Imagine a truck that was packed with diamonds or goods the world needs. The truck drives into a camp of refugees who need the water and the food in it, and yet the carrier refuses to offload and drives back to base.

That is how many people are. They came, they saw but they never delivered.

It is time to be a braveheart.

To be a braveheart, you must let go of the bubble wrap you have around you. Do not be afraid. Be the man you are. Be the human you are but go out and 'break a leg'. Do the impossible.

Like Jesus, turn water to wine in your own way. Be a 'wild joy' person. Let people know that the joy you have has nothing to do with happiness that come from happenings.

"whom having not seen you love. Though now you do not see Him, yet believing, you rejoice with joy inexpressible and full of glory," 1 Peter 1:8

Be a braveheart. Be a gift embracer, which means you celebrate people who are gifted. Those are bravehearts. They are not jealous. They stand shoulder to shoulder with other people.

"The guards stood shoulder to shoulder: six Levites per day on the east, four per day on the north and on the south, and two at a time at the storehouse. At the open court to the west, four guards were posted on the road and two at the court." 1 Chronicles 26:16-18 (The Message)

Let us conclude this chapter by saying that in a world of cowardice, in a world where Christians are compromising and running away from truth, refusing to defend their faith, while we see a people who believe a lie and are ready to die for it; be the one who looks life in the face and says, "I am a braveheart. You cannot beat me."

Do it the way Christians bravehearts would do it. Those who are believers know that love is risky and yet, they reach out and love anyway. Those who are bravehearts still believe in the impossible, even when they know it is impossible.

"But Jesus looked at them and said to them, "With men this is impossible, but with God all things are possible."" Matthew 19:26

It is time to be a braveheart

Be a braveheart. Be a person who fights like they are unstoppable. And truly, you are unstoppable.

"Fight the good fight of faith, lay hold on eternal life, to which you were also called and have confessed the good confession in the presence of many witnesses." 1 Timothy 6:12

Be a braveheart who never gives in, who never gives up and who never lets go. Chase Jesus with a tender world-changing wildness so when anyone sees the way you love the Lord and speak for Him, they will know you are a braveheart.

Fearless Faith

CONQUERORS

"So, what do you think? With God on our side like this, how can we lose? If God didn't hesitate to put everything on the line for us, embracing our condition and exposing himself to the worst by sending his own Son, is there anything else he wouldn't gladly and freely do for us? And who would dare tangle with God by messing with one of God's chosen? Who would dare even to point a finger? The One who died for us—who was raised to life for us! — Is in the presence of God at this very moment sticking up for us. Do you think anyone is going to be able to drive a wedge between us and Christ's love for us? There is no way! Not trouble, not hard times, not hatred, not hunger, not homelessness, not bullying threats, not backstabbing, not even the worst sins listed in Scripture: they kill us in cold blood because they hate you. We're sitting ducks; they pick us off one by one. None of this fazes us because Jesus loves us. I'm absolutely convinced that nothing—

nothing living or dead, angelic or demonic, today or tomorrow, high or low, thinkable or unthinkable— absolutely nothing can get between us and God's love because of the way that Jesus our Master has embraced us." Romans 8:31-39 (The Message)

The Bible, in both the Old and New Testaments, is full of the language of battles and conquests. The passage quoted above shows that Paul reckons that Christianity is a battlefield and until we win and leave this earth, the battle never ceases.

The danger for the Body of Christ would be to be at ease in Zion.

"Woe to you who are at ease in Zion, and trust in Mount Samaria, notable persons in the chief nation, to whom the house of Israel comes!" Amos 6:1

We would be pretentious to say that there is no battle around us; against our faith. There is a battle because of our faith and our pursuit of the life that we have chosen to live in Christ Jesus.

This must be the reason why Paul summarised by saying, *"Nay, in all these things we are more than conquerors."*

We could list a thousand and one things for which the believer must find grace to become a conqueror but, for the sake of brevity, we will look at only a few.

1. Negative Reports

> The danger for the Body of Christ would be to be at ease in Zion

"But the men who had gone up with him said, "We are not able to go up against the people, for they are stronger than we." And they gave the children of Israel a bad report of the land which they had spied out, saying, "The land through which we have gone as spies is a land that devours its inhabitants, and all the people whom we saw in it are men of great stature." Numbers 13:31-32

The children of Israel had already stepped out of Egypt and were on their way to the Promised Land but between departure and arrival there would be a battle. They would have to learn to become conquerors.

The first battle is not physical per say but, rather one of words. Words that can either strengthen the mind or weaken it.

Negative reports were used to douse the mind of the people of God and it resulted in the majority of those who left Egypt not making it to the Promised Land.

These are the days of giants

In the twenty-first century, the advent of social media and various platforms for expressing one's opinion has given people who do not support our faith, or even those who behave like the fifth column within the faith, to attack, belittle, malign and make a negative impact on it .

Some have gone as far as writing things that are completely ludicrous, false and unimaginable. Even though there may be warnings that one should take everything that comes various social media platforms with a pinch of salt, once the eye gate is used to see, read and imbibe, the heart tends to believe.

The rate of attack on ministries and ministers, based on these platforms and the information we get from them, the questioning of certain major teachings of the Body of Christ like tithing, virginity, the trinity etc... has meant that the Church has not noticed that the very platforms which have given us the opportunity to spread the Gospel far and wide, have been turned around as a weapon to fight the church.

We need conquerors who will rise undaunted and not allow these things to stop them.

2. Giants

"There we saw the giants (the descendants of Anak came from the giants); and we were like grasshoppers in our own sight, and so we were in their sight." Number 13:33

In Numbers 13:33, the Children of Israel came across giants. Giants are a symbol of oppositions and challenges of the day, impossible things the believer has to face. In today's world delegated authority, such as governments are becoming so averse to Christianity. In the Western Hemisphere it is much easier for other religions to get approval for their places of worship than it is for a church. And if a church were to get permission, after a lot of intense battle, gathering money and buying an old disused industrial site, even in the city where there are several industrial sites that have been shut down, a church can still be resisted by the planning authorities on the premise that converting the site to a place of worship is a 'loss of industrial space'. In the United States the law of the eminent domain has meant that churches have been refused permission to build in an area.

These are the days of giants. The whole Charter of the European Union binding all of the European nations excludes the word 'God.'

We face giants. We need believers who will realise it is not play time. It is power and prayer time.

3. Fear

"Only do not rebel against the Lord, nor fear the people of the land, for they are our bread; their protection has departed from them, and the Lord is with us. Do not fear them." Numbers 14:9

We may not deal with this in much detail here but in another chapter, however, this unspoken enemy has made the Church become more of a defender or apologiser for what we believe, rather than fighting for what we stand for.

Fear of the unknown, fear of being misunderstood, fear of being criticised, the fear of being considered to be different will make many churches never speak against certain social mores.

Fear is a tormentor. Fear takes away the joy of following Christ. it is not the spirit that comes from God.

"For God has not given us a spirit of fear, but of power and of love and of a sound mind." 2 Timothy 1:7

4. Tears

"So all the congregation lifted up their voices and cried, and the people wept that night." Numbers 14:1

The worst battle of life is the one we do not understand

Fear and torment will lead to tears. They will lead to the belief that things have fallen apart and there cannot be a change. The feeling of despondency can make a person not exercise the mantle of a conqueror.

The time has come for the Church to awaken and realise that if anyone must cry, it is not us and if we must cry, it is in the presence of the Lord in worship and celebration of Him.

5. Chariots of iron

"So the Lord was with Judah. And they drove out the mountaineers, but they could not drive out the inhabitants of the lowland, because they had chariots of iron." Judges 1:19

The Children of Israel had met with many kinds of obstacles. The majority of them were not unfamiliar, however, chariots of iron was a new strategy of the enemy to belittle the people of God and make them cower in the presence of their enemies.

You can break satanic walls. They must not hold you

The worst battle of life is the one we do not understand. The passage quoted shows that while the Children of Israel had mastery and victory over everyone including mountaineers, they could not drive out the inhabitants of lowlands who had chariots of iron.

This was their experience; however, we have a comfort in the fact that the scripture tells us that before the battle began, we are more than conquerors.

6. Wars

"Now Jericho was securely shut up because of the children of Israel; none went out, and none came in."
Joshua 6:1

On a particular visit to Jerusalem, when I had gone to preach for God TV, I took the time for a guide to show my wife and I around the city of Jerusalem. We came upon the wall of Hezekiah, which looked like it was three meters wide. This was the wall that surrounded Jerusalem in the days of Hezekiah. Yet, a wall of three meters in width was not anything compared to the walls of Jericho.

Walls are built because the enemy is trying to frustrate you. He is scared of your coming glory. Walls can be thrown at you at any time. The walls of personal experience, the walls of insecurity, fear, walls which try to veil you off from favour, walls of mere survival instead of enjoying your faith, walls of building a defence mechanism instead of taking territories and possessing possessions, walls of satanic intimidation or those of self-imprisonment, walls that lock up the blessings of God or hinder from the glory of the Lord, walls that make a man unable to taste the blessings of God.

Wherever these walls are coming from and whatever they are made of, you can overcome them. You can break satanic walls. They must not hold you.

The attempt is to contain, to retain and to frustrate. We need conquerors who see the battle but are unafraid of it.

7. Battles

In the verse we quoted earlier, Joshua 6:1, it says, *"Jericho was securely shut."* But, remember it was not shut until the Children of Israel came.

Every time Kingdom people make up their mind to be conquerors and take territories, satan jumps. Crisis always occurs at the curve of change. Battles always surround the birth of a miracle, but the battle can also introduce you to the blessing.

Conquerors never give up because a battle arises. They see the chance to shine. When David, who had the spirit of a conqueror, saw Goliath, he did not throw in the towel and run away. He accepted the challenge to confront the giant.

For the sake of this book, we will say that the opposite of being a conqueror, is actually being a coward. Cowards follow the path of least resistance. Conquerors look for a place to shine for God.

Ahab, the king, was a man who had this spirit of least resistance. He allowed Jezebel to put him under her control. Cowards follow the voice of the majority. Ten of the twelve spies (Numbers 13 and 14) may have been crowd followers. Once the crowd was up in arms and in tears, the people could not hold their stand and say, "we must go and conquer."

It is better to be a radical, lonely conqueror full of the Spirit, than a coward who gives up his inheritance in the face of battles.

Conquerors never give up because a battle arises. They see the chance to shine.

Cowards are fuelled by fear. Conquerors are fuelled by faith. Imagine that a man with Christmas crackers has the power to scare you, while you have Molotov cocktails, grenades and bombs.

Christians have the weapons of God. Satan has only a Christmas cracker. The God who used David's sling, will bring down Goliath for you. You have someone who fights your battles. That is why Paul said, "We are more than conquerors."

Conquerors win, but when you are more than a conqueror, it means that you are not just a heavy-weight champion, you are more because the one who backs you is too much for the one who fights you.

Cowards depend on their own works. We rely on the Word of God. Cowards boast in what their weapons will do. We make our boast in the Word of God and what it will do; declaring that is it is sharper than any sword.

We have not been called to cowardice

"For the word of God is living and powerful, and sharper than any two-edged sword, piercing even to the division of soul and spirit, and of joints and marrow, and is a discerner of the thoughts and intents of the heart." Hebrews 4:12

Cowards are cry-babies. In the face of the slightest confrontation, a church, its leaders and individuals demonstrate cowardice and apologise for the faith they once held so proudly, simply because it is now against the tide.

"So all the congregation lifted up their voices and cried, and the people wept that night." Numbers 14:1

Conquerors are willing to be misunderstood. I personally believe that some of the saints of whom we read, who gave up their life and became martyrs, were conquerors.

Cowards live in the past. Conquerors see a glorious future. It is interesting to notice that cowards and conquerors had the opportunity to see the same thing. If we look at the story in Numbers 13, of the twelve men who went to Canaan, all of them saw the good land, but ten chose to give a bad report. All of them saw the bounty, but ten came back empty handed. All of them saw the material blessing, but ten returned to talk about the challenges. All of them saw the social opportunities, but ten came back to talk about the negative consequences of moving forward. All of them saw the spiritual benefits of God providing, protecting and promoting, but ten returned and said their God was too small and that they were like grasshoppers before the enemy.

"There we saw the giants (the descendants of Anak came from the giants); and we were like grasshoppers in our own sight, and so we were in their sight." Number 13:33

We have not been called to cowardice. We are not the ones who turn our back to the attacks of the enemy. We have the Spirit of a conqueror and even much more because we have been called to be more than conquerors. The power we talk of does not come from us. It comes from the Lord. That is why death or life cannot overcome us. Height or depth, things present or to come, today or tomorrow, are not enough to scare a man who has a conqueror's mantle.

The battle is raging in our world. The various avenues for attacking the church have increased. The Press is not friendly. Television is not on our side. Government policies and various social media platforms are not favourable to the Gospel of Christ. However, yes, in all these things, we are more than conquerors.

WHAT SHOULD THE CONQUEROR DO TO DEMONSTRATE A FEARLESS FAITH AND TAKE BACK LOST TERRITORIES?

1. We must start living for Christ

Paul said, *"For to me, to live is Christ, and to die is gain."* *Philippians 1:21*

There must be a clear distinction between those who know the Lord and those who do not.

"Therefore, if anyone is in Christ, he is a new creation; old things have passed away; behold, all things have become new." 2 Corinthians 5:17

We are born of heaven. We are overcoming children of an overcoming God. We now have the nature of a loving God. We did not embrace religion. We embraced a relationship with a living, dynamic, resurrected Christ. If we have to stop living for things to show our conquests, we might as well. In the words of Jim Elliot, "He is no fool who gives what he cannot keep to gain what he cannot lose.[1]"

Living for Christ means that we must know that now in Him, all things have become new.

We embraced a relationship with a living, dynamic, resurrected Christ

"Therefore, if anyone is in Christ, he is a new creation; old things have passed away; behold, all things have become new." 2 Corinthians 5:17

And this "new" would need to be shown. He is the One who said, He makes all things new.

"Behold, I will do a new thing, now it shall spring forth; shall you not know it? I will even make a road in the wilderness and rivers in the desert. The beast of the field will honor Me, the jackals and the ostriches, because I give waters in the wilderness and rivers in the desert, to give drink to My people, My chosen." Isaiah 43:19-20

To live for Christ means to draw closer to Him. That is where we draw the strength from, the One who conquered death and hell. Failure to live in Christ or live in the Spirit therefore means walking in the flesh, surrendering to flesh and allowing it to make us the same as a person who has been conquered by the world.

"I say then: Walk in the Spirit, and you shall not fulfill the lust of the flesh." Galatians 5:16

We have not been called to cowardice

"But if you are led by the Spirit, you are not under the law." Galatians 5: 18

"If we live in the Spirit, let us also walk in the Spirit." Galatians 5:25

When we do not live for Christ, we stop praying, we stop searching the Word, we stop fellowshipping with the believers.

"Not forsaking the assembling of ourselves together, as is the manner of some, but exhorting one another, and so much the more as you see the Day approaching." Hebrews 10:25

We are called to be in fellowship to draw strength from one another.

Conquerors live for Christ. Conquerors are like the sunflower. When the sun is bright, the sunflower turns its large face upwards to draw energy, but when the day is dark and dull and there is no sun from which to draw, it faces other sunflowers and they draw strength from one another. Our fellowship is to worship the Lord, but to also draw strength.

2. We must lean on Christ

To lean on anything else would be disastrous.

"Trust in the Lord with all your heart, and lean not on your own understanding;" Proverbs 3:5

Today's world is directed and led by people who put their trust in their cerebral capacities. We are not fools or brainless, but we totally lean on Him because we know that He knows best.

In the words of John Calvin, "There is no other method of living piously and justly, than that of depending upon God.[2]"

Leaning on Him must be implicit, total and without reservation. Your life will not change if you depend on yourself. We must trust the Lord for direction.

"In all your ways acknowledge Him, and He shall direct your paths." Proverbs 3:6

When a man depends on God, nothing will be impossible. There will be a way out, even where they say there is no way. He is the One who created the universe and made some things which, until the time comes, we see no way in them. He made it!

We must acknowledge that we are not capable of guiding ourselves. There are questions you can never answer. You do not know the day you will die. You do not know when you will die. You do not know what time you will die. You do not know where you will die. You do not know how you will die because you are finite.

But, when we depend on Him, we find help and hope. If God is all you have, then you have all you need. You cannot depend on God and say you do not have anything.

"Philip said to Him, "Lord, show us the Father, and it is sufficient for us.""John 14:8

Dependence on God is not a weakness. It is the acknowledgement of His strength. Of course, this does not mean swinging the pendulum so far to the point where we say we are just so totally dependent on God that we do not think for ourselves. He has given us sanctified minds to be able to know when He is leading.

What we are saying is do not put your trust in man. To be a conqueror you must totally lean on the Lord, not even on your strength. When David confronted his enemies, though a man of war, he sought the mind of God, to know if he should go on.

"Now when the Philistines heard that they had anointed David king over Israel, all the Philistines went up to search for David. And David heard of it and went down to the stronghold. The Philistines also went and deployed

themselves in the Valley of Rephaim. So David inquired of the Lord, saying, "Shall I go up against the Philistines? Will You deliver them into my hand?" And the Lord said to David, "Go up, for I will doubtless deliver the Philistines into your hand." So David went to Baal Perazim, and David defeated them there; and he said, "The Lord has broken through my enemies before me, like a breakthrough of water." Therefore he called the name of that place Baal Perazim." 2 Samuel 5:17-20

If God is all you have, then you have all you need

Even your own shadow disappears when you are in darkness. The Lord helps believers and saves His children. So, the key to happiness is not to be in someone else's pocket but to put yourself totally in the hand of God and lean on Him.

3. We must labour for Christ

The third way to demonstrate your conquest and the Spirit of a conqueror is to labour for Christ. Enough of Christians who want to sneak into heaven incognito.

We must identify with Him in labouring for Him here on earth, populating heaven and de-populating hell.

It is what we do for Christ that will last

"We then, as workers together with Him also plead with you not to receive the grace of God in vain" 2 Corinthians 6:1

There is no other wisdom, but that shown in drawing men out of hell and winning them to Christ. He who wins souls is wise.

"The fruit of the righteous is a tree of life, and he who wins souls is wise." Proverbs 11:30

It is while we are busy serving the Lord, not caring which prayer has been answered, that the answer comes following after us.

"As each one has received a gift, minister it to one another, as good stewards of the manifold grace of God." 1 Peter 4:10

"Only fear the Lord, and serve Him in truth with all your heart; for consider what great things He has done for you." 1 Samuel 12:24

Let us labour for Him in soul winning and ministry, getting people to know Christ and proclaiming Him to the whole world; and let us do it with diligence. Some already serve, but they are not hard, diligent workers. Let us serve, as if all our life depends on it. Mark 10:45.

"For even the Son of Man did not come to be served, but to serve, and to give His life a ransom for many."" Mark 10:45

Many complain of the lack of time and concern and they do not realise, if you do not have time now, what happens if sickness finds you and you are at the vestibule of eternity? Make time to serve the Lord. That is what we are taught to do, seek Him first.

"But seek first the kingdom of God and His righteousness, and all these things shall be added to you." Matthew 6:33

Conquerors must labour by speaking a kind word to someone who needs to know that contrary to some of the funny images of Christ and Christianity painted in our world today, He is still the reason for living.

"If anyone speaks, let him speak as the oracles of God. If anyone ministers, let him do it as with the ability which God supplies, that in all things God may be glorified through Jesus Christ, to whom belong the glory and the dominion forever and ever. Amen." 1 Peter 4:11

Let us reach out and give assistance to those who need it. Let us witness to the lost. It is time to make our own time count by serving the Lord. It is what we do for Christ that will last.

"I must work the works of Him who sent Me while it is day; the night is coming when no one can work." John 9:4

When we get to eternity, we will not be asked how many people we knew, which places we visited or how many houses we owned. What will count in eternity is the souls who came to know Christ through us.

4. We must love through Christ

Conquerors are also very loving through Christ. Our world has become totally lopsided. There is so much hatred. Since the killing of Abel by Cain, our planet has only known eighteen years of 'no bloodshed' according to Bible scholars.

It is the song which occupies our radio waves. It is the song that makes the biggest hit and yet the love of which people sing today is not the love of 'giving you in spite of.' It is not agape, unconditional. It is a love that speaks of what they will do to another person's body, what a man will do to a woman, what a woman will do with a man.

Conquerors know that in a world full of hatred, children taken advantage of, raped, maimed, molested and of family violence, what the world needs to see is genuine and true love.

"And walk in love, as Christ also has loved us and given Himself for us, an offering and a sacrifice to God for a sweet-smelling aroma." Ephesians 5:2

Christians often fail to walk in this kind of love, when we shouldn't. Our kind of conquest is not shown by the sword we draw. We do not burn down the house of those who do not accept our faith. We do not slaughter, kill and destroy anyone who tuns their back on Christianity. We keep loving them until they see that a loving God would rather give them love than hatred.

What will count in eternity is the souls who came to know Christ through us

"This is My commandment, that you love one another as I have loved you. Greater love has no one than this, than to lay down one's life for his friends." John 15:12-13

So, this true love is giving oneself for others, being more like Jesus, exhibiting less drama, complaining less, expressing less bitterness, not gossiping, not being so proud and being true in loving those who need to know Christ.

"bears all things, believes all things, hopes all things, endures all things." 1 Corinthians 13:7

This God-kind of love must be shown to believers and also to unbelievers. When we show it to believers, they increase. When we show it to the unsaved, they realise they have a choice to know the Son of God.

Conquerors must know that the Lord will fight for them

"And this is His commandment: that we should believe on the name of His Son Jesus Christ and love one another, as He gave us commandment." 1 John 3:23

In opening this chapter, we looked a lot at what happened to the Children of Israel and the battles they had to confront as they became conquerors, even though they were just pilgrims travelling to an unknown land. God guaranteed their victory - if they would do a few things.

Let us close this chapter by saying, the conquerors who will be fearless in faith must:

1. Sanctify their own mind

"Then Joshua circumcised their sons whom He raised up in their place; for they were uncircumcised, because they had not been circumcised on the way. So it was, when they had finished circumcising all the people, that they stayed in their places in the camp till they were healed." Joshua 5:7-8

Put away the flesh. Make a clear break with the lifestyle that does not honour Christ and walk in the Spirit.

You cannot enter your land of conquest without circumcising what represents fleshly living.

2. Strengthen themselves

"And the Lord said to Joshua, "Do not fear them, for I have delivered them into your hand; not a man of them shall stand before you."" Joshua 10:8

"Be strong and of good courage, for to this people you shall divide as an inheritance the land which I swore to their fathers to give them. Only be strong and very courageous, that you may observe to do according to all the law which Moses My servant commanded you; do not turn from it to the right hand or to the left, that you may prosper wherever you go." Joshua 1:6-7

"Have I not commanded you? Be strong and of good courage; do not be afraid, nor be dismayed, for the Lord your God is with you wherever you go."" Joshua 1:9

Conquerors must know that the Lord will fight for them. They will not be alone in the battle of life.

"And it came to pass, when Joshua was by Jericho, that he lifted his eyes and looked, and behold, a Man stood opposite him with His sword drawn in His hand. And Joshua went to Him and said to Him, "Are You for us or for our adversaries?" So He said, "No, but as Commander of the army of the Lord I have now come." And Joshua fell on his face to the earth and worshiped, and said to Him, "What does my Lord say to His servant?" Then the Commander of the Lord's army said to Joshua, "Take your sandal off your foot, for the place where you stand is holy." And Joshua did so." Joshua 5:13-15

We have written a lot about social media and the attacks that come against the Body of Christ. The conqueror must know the power of silence, the time to be silent and not respond to those who attack because silence cannot be misquoted. Silence protects your focus. Your words can be used in evidence against you. Your goal is to finish well. Your enemy's goal is to abort your vision, your dream, your destiny. So, there is a time when silence is the weapon, when the enemy will not be able to quote you; and there is a time when the words to speak are totally different from what they expect from you.

"A soft answer turns away wrath, but a harsh word stirs up anger." Proverbs 15:1

Conquerors must see the victory ahead when it is oblivious to others.

"And the Lord said to Joshua: "See! I have given Jericho into your hand, its king, and the mighty men of valour." Joshua 6:2

You must see Jericho already fallen in your mind. That is what makes you a conqueror, a person who will win.

3. Wait for the perfect time

Conquerors must now know how to wait for the perfect time. God told the children of Israel to go round city seven times.

> So, there is a time when silence is the weapon, when the enemy will not be able to quote you

"And seven priests shall bear seven trumpets of rams' horns before the ark. But the seventh day you shall march around the city seven times, and the priests shall blow the trumpets." Joshua 6:4

Seven is the number of perfection. Many times, we feel the time is now, but true conquerors know the time is determined by the One who has a fuller picture. You can only see from three or four dimensions. He sees all the dimensions and He knows the perfect time.

4. Know how to shout

Finally, conquerors must know how to shout and manifest the spirit of conquest.

"So the people shouted when the priests blew the trumpets. And it happened when the people heard the sound of the trumpet, and the people shouted with a great shout, that the wall fell down flat. Then the people went up into the city, every man straight before him, and they took the city." Joshua 6:20

When you shout, life's complications disappear. You cannot praise God and be stranded on the highway of life.

---

[1] https://www.brainyquote.com/quotes/jim_elliot_189244

[2] https://twitter.com/johncalvindaily/
status/667770521371545600

CHAMPIONS LEAGUE PEOPLE

Who is a champion?

The best definition of a champion is a person who has overcome all rivals in a sporting context or competition.

This in effect means that if there has not been any winning, to call oneself a champion would be an aberration.

The calling and disposition of believers of fearless faith is to realise that Christianity is not a call to failure or to be a victim. It is a calling to win in life.

God will not set you up to fail. There is no sign of Him doing that. Every provision He has made is for your success.

The context in which we use the word 'champion' to describe Christians of fearless faith is of them being advocates of that which is right in a world of unrighteousness; they are promoters of truth; people who plead for the right thing; carriers of the torch who will not allow pessimism or their own weariness to stop them.

Champions of the faith are protectors of territory, upholders of the truth, supporters of what is right, backers of righteousness. They are people who have had to battle in defence of the faith, who will go out on a crusade to promote the righteousness of Jesus Christ, who will take up the cudgels and cut through until there is a victory and a testimony for the cause of Jesus Christ.

> **Before the athlete wins in public, he has won in private**

Champions do not surrender to opposition. They do not allow critics to cut them down and reduce their dream. Let us look in more detail at those who are in the Champions League.

"And the things that you have heard from me among many witnesses, commit these to faithful men who will be able to teach others also. You therefore must endure

hardship as a good soldier of Jesus Christ. No one engaged in warfare entangles himself with the affairs of this life, that he may please him who enlisted him as a soldier." 2 Timothy 2:2-4

"Therefore I endure all things for the sake of the elect, that they also may obtain the salvation which is in Christ Jesus with eternal glory." 2 Timothy 2:10

In 2 Timothy, Paul presents to us three kinds of professions that require certain attitudes in order to win: Soldiers, farmers and athletes all require discipline. It is the discipline of an athlete that makes him stand out and win. Before the athlete wins in public, he has won in private. It is the discipline of the soldier that makes him enables him to not be carried away by civilian life. It is the discipline of the farmer that enables him to wait for the harvest after he has planted.

We all carry the seed of championship in us, the seed of greatness, irrespective of what we face. For that champion to manifest, certain qualities must exist. Let us consider some of the qualities necessary for the believer to shift and become a champion in the champions' league,

WHAT ARE THE THINGS THAT MAKE CHAMPIONS STAND OUT?

1. They do not make excuses

They find a way. Excuse-making is the mantra of the lazy. The lazy will complain that there is a lion on the way when they are supposed to go hunting.

"The lazy man says, "There is a lion outside! I shall be slain in the streets!"" Proverbs 22:13

No athlete can become a world champion without bruises and pains because they will have had to stretch their body beyond the regular. It was said of Evander Holyfield that a couple of days after beating Mike Tyson and earning fifteen million dollars, he was out again, exercising and doing road-running because he knew that while he may have received the reward of that fight, he still needed to be in shape to win the next one..

Champions accept the responsibility for their spiritual life and for their destination. They choose not to blame someone else. It is very easy to play the blame game. Adam did, he blamed Eve. Eve did, she blamed the serpent. And since our first parents, Adam and Eve, mankind has always played the blame game.

2. They surround themselves with people on the same mission as they are

> Excuse-making is the mantra of the lazy

Your association will determine your assimilation. Who you move with determines what you see, hear and believe. Who you hear determines who hears you. Wrong associates provoke bad decisions. Many people who have ended up in all kinds of vices – prostitution, drug addiction, walking away from the faith, a degradation of their moral standards – have done so mainly because of wrong associations.

When you choose quality associations, you raise the quality of your achievements. Paul expresses painfully the consequence of moving with the wrong crowd.

> *"For many walk, of whom I have told you often, and now tell you even weeping, that they are the enemies of the cross of Christ" Philippians 3:18*

> *"Reject a divisive man after the first and second admonition," Titus 3:10*

3. They know that if they fail to plan, they plan to fail

Criticism is the only contribution the failed, the nonchalant and the laid back give to those who succeed

"The plans of the diligent lead surely to plenty, but those of everyone who is hasty, surely to poverty." Proverbs 21:5

You cannot be a champion if you have no clearly defined goals and direction for your life. With goals, there is a going. Without goals, there would be no goals scored. Champions are not rated in any game because they simply showed up. They are champions because they won.

4. They pay for whatever they order

Lifestyles have consequences. If you subscribe to a life of discipline, you receive the consequences of discipline: the benefits and fruits that follow. If you subscribe to a life of inconsistency in your thinking, being unfocused in your journey, devoid of convictions in your belief system, you will also reap the consequences.

Lifestyles have consequences. Things do not just happen. Our choices determine our chances. Look around you. Bring to remembrance people whom you appreciate and celebrate. Think of the price they may have paid to reach the place they have attained today. Certain choices were made that brought about the chances they have.

5. They learn something positive from every criticism

Criticism is the only contribution the failed, the nonchalant and the laid back give to those who succeed.

If you must be a champion you must be ready for criticism and when it is thrown at you, you must see it as a chance to use it to grow.

"The ear that hears the rebukes of life will abide among the wise. He who disdains instruction despises his own soul, but he who heeds rebuke gets understanding." *Proverbs 15:31-32*

Criticism can become a good teacher, a good tool, a good weapon, and a good opportunity to grow. It can become what you use to climb higher. One person's criticism is another person's source of blessing. One snowy day, a cow that consumed a lot of hay excretes a large amount of waste. Unknown to the cow, its waste falls on top of a bird that is nearly frozen to death. This warm excretion that fell on the bird became the bird's lifesaver. So, one person's waste can become another person's blessing.

The criticisms thrown at you can become your reason for growing into a champion.

6. They constantly innovate and stay relevant

Our world is changing. The environment is changing. Nations are changing. Things around us are changing. Nothing ever remains the same. Our generation has experienced more change than any other. The things we used to know have metamorphosed several times within a short time.

Fearless faith requires that you know how to be innovative, stay relevant and keep abreast of the facts. Christianity does not call us to live a life of backwardness, being stuck in some dark age. We are called to be relevant and renewed.

"Any enterprise is built by wise planning, becomes strong through common sense, and profits wonderfully by keeping abreast of the facts." Proverbs 24:3-4 (Living Bible - TLB)

7. They perform like they have never lost. They practice like they have never won

I quoted the story of Evander Holyfield earlier, who, only two days after winning a boxing bout against Mike Tyson with a price tag of fifteen million dollars, was back to his exercise as if he had never won.

The feeling of arrival can stop you from arriving.

The criticisms thrown at you can become your reason for growing into a champion

> *"Not that I have already attained, or am already perfected; but I press on, that I may lay hold of that for which Christ Jesus has also laid hold of me. Brethren, I do not count myself to have apprehended; but one thing I do, forgetting those things which are behind and reaching forward to those things which are ahead, 14 I press toward the goal for the prize of the upward call of God in Christ Jesus." Philippians 3:12-14*

Too many people announce victory too early. They settle for the immediate when there could have been more to discover. Imagine the two apostles who ran to the tomb of Jesus at the Resurrection. John, the younger one, got there first. On seeing the empty tomb, he did not go in, perhaps thinking it was over but Peter did not only see an empty tomb, he went in, took the time to examine it and found a nicely folded shroud. This act meant that the one who was even slower, the one who took more time, discovered more.

Who knows, John, being younger, may have had the mind of "whoever runs to the tomb and gets there first is the winner!" Without realising that the race is not to the swift.

> In order for you to be in the league of champions quitting must not be in your dictionary

8. Quitting is not in their dictionary

The truth is quitters never win and winners never quit. Champions who have a fearless faith do not consider the option of quitting.

When some people left Jesus, after he chided them for pursuing mere food, He turned to His disciples and asked, "Will you also go away? And Peter responded,

"But Simon Peter answered Him, "Lord, to whom shall we go? You have the words of eternal life." John 6:68

It is said that when the Queen of Spain sent Herman Cortez to invade Mexico and conquer it in 1519. One of the strategies of the Spanish conquistador of the Aztec empire was to burn the eleven ships which brought him, his soldiers and the priests as soon they arrived in Mexico. It is said that the soldiers shouted and screamed, wondering how they would go back to Spain from this strange land. Herman Cortez told them, "It is very simple. Conquer Mexico, then you can build new ships that will take you back."

The lesson here was that as long as those boats were in the harbour, the soldiers were likely to fight with half-hearted devotion, knowing that there was always the option of returning to Spain.

Cortez burnt the ships to let everyone know that there was no going back, there was no giving in, there was no giving up.

In order for you to be in the league of champions quitting must not be in your dictionary.

9. They never complain but train to be better

In every game champions live a few years of their lives unlike 'normal' people. Most soccer players, in the early years avoid certain food, habits and places. They choose a particular life style and even sleeping pattern because it is required to keep them fit, focused, fighting and winning.

In the arena of athletics, many athletes are picky about their food, picky with their time and with everyone, preferring to hide in the back-woods and train because it takes only a few years of their life to make the name that will stay with them for a lifetime.

So, champions live a few years of their life unlike other people. Why? So, they can spend the rest of their life like most people do not.

At the time of the writing of this book, Usain Bolt was thirty-two years old with a net worth of sixteen million US dollars. Of his thirty-two years, probably close to sixteen of them were spent in the arduous task of remaining slim, hard and fast. Now that Bolt has accumulated such wealth, he is likely to live his life unlike most people his age.

Clearly this must make us realise it is not how long you live, but how well. It is not the number of days you live, but the life you gave and what you brought to the table.

Jesus only spent thirty-three years on earth, three intense years of ministry turned the world upside down and today, almost half of the world follows Him, either as committed believers or Christians by association. His first thirty years were silent, but the three years of ministry were intense and impactful.

10. Regardless of what tries to quench their faith, champions maintain their momentum

> It is not the number of days you live, but the life you gave and what you brought to the table

Moses was given instruction that the fire in the presence of the Lord must never go out. In other words, he had to keep the fire burning. Keeping the fire burning requires consecration.

> "A fire shall always be burning on the altar; it shall never go out." Leviticus 6:13

> "Then one of the seraphim flew to me, having in his hand a live coal which he had taken with the tongs from the altar. And he touched my mouth with it, and said: "Behold, this has touched your lips; your iniquity is taken away, and your sin purged."" Isaiah 6:6-7

Without consecration, Christianity becomes perfunctory and lacks power. To keep the fire burning requires dedication. You cannot be immunised from suffering when you are dedicated to the cause of Christ. You will have to face something, but you will have a testimony.

> "Then the mother of Zebedee's sons came to Him with her sons, kneeling down and asking something from Him. And He said to her, "What do you wish?" She said to Him,

> **To keep the fire burning may mean purging to remove what does not honour God**

"Grant that these two sons of mine may sit, one on Your right hand and the other on the left, in Your kingdom." But Jesus answered and said, "You do not know what you ask. Are you able to drink the cup that I am about to drink, and be baptized with the baptism that I am baptized with?" They said to Him, "We are able." So He said to them, "You will indeed drink My cup, and be baptized with the baptism that I am baptized with; but to sit on My right hand and on My left is not Mine to give, but it is for those for whom it is prepared by My Father."" Matthew 20:20-23

Your flesh may not like the pit and may hate the challenges, but champions keep the fire burning. They know what is required.

To keep the fire burning may mean you must be ready for consumption. Champions are consumed by zeal for God. They are consumed by their desire to serve Him. They are consumed by the impact they want to make like. They allow their works to reveal their person.

To keep the fire burning means you know that you must get ready for perfection.

""Behold, I have created the blacksmith who blows the coals in the fire, who brings forth an instrument for his

work; and I have created the spoiler to destroy."
Isaiah 54:16

To keep the fire burning may mean purging to remove what does not honour God, in order for you to truly be a champion, really make the impact and touch your world.

Keeping the fire burning can be summarised by the words of Sylvester Stallone who said, "I am not the richest, smartest or most talented person in the world, but I succeed because I keep going and going and going."

That is what we mean by "Keeping the fire burning." It means that irrespective of the obstacles, people in the champions' league are never stopped. If there is an obstacle they do not even know it.

Pilots do not refuse to fly if they anticipate a bump or storm ahead. They know there will be turbulence. However, they also know that the fuselage of the plane they fly has been built for resilience.

11. They seek for the keys that unlock the realms of success

The most powerful key for those in the faith was given to Joshua, as he took the place of Moses.

"This Book of the Law shall not depart from your mouth, but you shall meditate in it day and night, that you may observe to do according to all that is written in it. For then you will make your way prosperous, and then you will have good success." Joshua 1:8

Moses was such a colossal figure that it was difficult to replace him. He was highly educated, highly spiritual, highly tested and of an unusual stock and yet Joshua was called to fill the shoes of his boss. In calling Joshua, God also gave him the secret for joining the champions' league: "the Word should not depart from his mouth". As long as Joshua kept the Word of God as the blueprint for his journey, he would make it to the other side.

We need people who will not be ashamed or afraid in this twenty-first century, we need people who realise and recognise the relevance of biblical truth as the reason for true success.

12. They always keep their end result within sight

> We need people who realise and recognise the relevance of biblical truth as the reason for true success

The end result is a good motivator, so when the body calls for rest, you know it's not yet time to rest. When the mind says you have done too much, the end result spurs you on, that there is still one more step, one more action, one more way.

> *"Looking unto Jesus, the author and finisher of our faith, who for the joy that was set before Him endured the cross, despising the shame, and has sat down at the right hand of the throne of God." Hebrews 12:2*

When you read the catalogue of the things Paul had to face for the sake of the Gospel, it is enough to discourage anyone.

> *"Are they Hebrews? So am I. Are they Israelites? So am I. Are they the seed of Abraham? So am I. Are they ministers of Christ? - I speak as a fool—I am more: in labors more abundant, in stripes above measure, in prisons more frequently, in deaths often. From the Jews five times I received forty stripes minus one. Three times I was beaten with rods; once I was stoned; three times I was shipwrecked; a night and a day I have been in the deep;*

> *in journeys often, in perils of waters, in perils of robbers, in perils of my own countrymen, in perils of the Gentiles, in perils in the city, in perils in the wilderness, in perils in the sea, in perils among false brethren; in weariness and toil, in sleeplessness often, in hunger and thirst, in fastings often, in cold and nakedness—besides the other things, what comes upon me daily: my deep concern for all the churches. Who is weak, and I am not weak? Who is made to stumble, and I do not burn with indignation? If I must boast, I will boast in the things which concern my infirmity. The God and Father of our Lord Jesus Christ, who is blessed forever, knows that I am not lying. In Damascus the governor, under Aretas the king, was guarding the city of the Damascenes with a garrison, desiring to arrest me; but I was let down in a basket through a window in the wall, and escaped from his hands." 2 Corinthians 11:22-33*

You must not be found associating with featherweight ideas when you have been upgraded to heavyweight championship

Paul had the end result in the mind. He wanted to be able to announce that he had fought a good fight and finished well.

> *"And let us not grow weary while doing good, for in due season we shall reap if we do not lose heart." Galatians 6:9*

13. Champions league persons are always upgrading mentally for the next level

Remember the scripture we quoted earlier.

"This Book of the Law shall not depart from your mouth, but you shall meditate in it day and night, that you may observe to do according to all that is written in it. For then you will make your way prosperous, and then you will have good success." Joshua 1:8

The Word of God is an upgrade. God makes it available for us to use it as the compass to navigate our world and reach the end of the journey. Those who are in the champions league know that the difference between the winner and the loser is the upgrade the winner gives themselves through the Word.

There are different levels of champions. You must not be found associating with featherweight ideas when you have been upgraded to heavyweight championship. Those who want to be in the category of heavyweight champions cannot allow featherweight matters to hold them down, put them down or limit them.

14. They have an "I have to do it, I need to do it" attitude

When you have a sense of necessity, it inspires a heightened motivation. When the attitude is, "I may not do it, I cannot do it, I will not do it," motivation and morale become low. When speaking about preaching of the Gospel Paul says,

"For if I preach the gospel, I have nothing to boast of, for necessity is laid upon me; yes, woe is me if I do not preach the gospel!" 1 Corinthians 9:16

In another passage, Paul says,

"Knowing, therefore, the terror of the Lord, we persuade men; but we are well known to God, and I also trust are well known in your consciences." 2 Corinthians 5:11

In this case, Paul's personal identity was attached to the ministry, to the Gospel. It is this personal identification that made him ready to pay the price – whatever it was. This is why Paul said,

"For to me, to live is Christ, and to die is gain." Philippians 1:21

This is how people in the champions league think. They think differently, talk differently and act differently. They do not come to the faith with an attitude of a paid employee; of someone who only came as a job-seeker. They own the dream. They live the dream and walk the dream.

> They think differently, talk differently and act differently

Christianity needs to come out of its current crisis by raising up a group of believers who are not in church because they need to get God 'off their back', or because they need to satisfy their conscience that they have been to church on a Sunday. We need people who weave their faith into their nine-to-five jobs and see a necessity for the Gospel to be more prevalent in every area of life.

15. They adopt and practice the disciplines of high achievers

Faith that is fearless, that is unperturbed by the threats in our world today will require the kind of discipline we see in high achievers.

Is our faith under threat? It certainly is. Across the globe there are churches, pastors and ministries that are be more afraid of ISIS attacking them or governments picking on them. They would rather hide their beliefs in order to stop people who hold certain sexual orientations from picking on them.

High achievers, in a nutshell, are disciplined, diligent, daring and determined.

There is no progress without change but not all change is progress

It is time for the Church to arise like a mighty warrior and take our place so the world knows we are not leaving this world like a quiet, timid bunch of people who have been fought into a corner. If we must leave, we will leave with a bang and while we are here, we will push the world to come to their knees at the feet of our Saviour.

16. They know good things take time

Champions are willing to wait.

When people become older, they can become complacent with age, but this does not deter champions. The older they become, the stronger and better they get.

If things need to change, the champions are ready to make it happen. There is no progress without change but not all change is progress. So, they look for the change that truly makes them win.

Paul talks of the patience that does a perfect work. He said,

"But let patience have its perfect work, that you may be perfect and complete, lacking nothing." James 1:4

David also said,

"I waited patiently for the Lord; and He inclined to me, and heard my cry. He also brought me up out of a horrible pit, out of the miry clay, and set my feet upon a rock, and established my steps. He has put a new song in my mouth, praise to our God; many will see it and fear, and will trust in the Lord." Psalm 40:1-3

17. They have grown with an innate knowledge that they were born for such a time as this

Believers who are in the champions league have this understanding.

"And He has made from one [a]blood every nation of men to dwell on all the face of the earth, and has determined their preappointed times and the boundaries of their dwellings, 27 so that they should seek the Lord, in the hope that they might grope for Him and find Him, though He is not far from each one of us; 28 for in Him we live and move and have our being, as also some of your own poets have said, 'For we are also His offspring.'" Acts 17:26-28

They know they are designated to achieve something. All of their experiences in life were meant to prepare them for where they are going. There is no doubt that God will back them up.

Everything about them was created to influence something and they are ready for conquest.

18. Champions league believers also know that God is calling them to do what they cannot do by themselves

It may take a battle or battles to get there but God will not permit things they cannot handle.

Joseph had to go through something to get there.

"They hurt his feet with fetters, he was laid in irons. Until the time that his word came to pass, the word of the Lord tested him." Psalm 105:18-19

Sometimes God will remove what will make things easily happen in order for the champion in you to truly manifest. Champions know that if there is a delay, it is because God wants you to be ready. He never manifests or makes a person who is a champions league individual fully manifest until the time is right.

God kept Joseph on hold for thirteen years in the obscurity of Egypt before a place was found for him as the Prime Minister. He kept Moses in the wilderness for forty years until he was ready to walk in the champions league. David was ordained at seventeen but did not fully occupy the throne of Israel until thirty years later.

> It may take a battle or battles to get there but God will not permit things they cannot handle

19. Champions league people also know that one must train to reign

They know that God will take you through the process of servanthood before the manifestation of kingship. Jesus Himself did that.

"Let this mind be in you which was also in Christ Jesus, who, being in the form of God, did not consider it robbery to be equal with God, but made Himself of no reputation, taking the form of a bondservant, and coming in the likeness of men. And being found in appearance as a man, He humbled Himself and became obedient to the point of death, even the death of the cross. Therefore God also has highly exalted Him and given Him the name which is above every name, that at the name of Jesus every knee should bow, of those in heaven, and of those on earth, and

> Championship is not about age; it is about stage and impact

of those under the earth, and that every tongue should confess that Jesus Christ is Lord, to the glory of God the Father." *Philippians 2:5-11*

In Christianity we do not start at the top, we start at the bottom. Jesus was a carpenter before He was manifested as a King. David was a shepherd before he became a king. Moses was a shepherd before he became a deliverer. Joseph was everything to the man whom he served but he went as low as being a slave before he rose to be who God called him to be.

20. Champions league believers know that they need to think tactically and operate strategically

Tactical thinking requires optimism, to be disciplined in disposition, compassionate in attitude towards people, with networking skills that can reach every man for the sake of Christ.

"For though I am free from all men, I have made myself a servant to all, that I might win the more; and to the Jews I became as a Jew, that I might win Jews; to those who are under the law, as under the law, that I might win those who are under the law; to those who are without

law, as without law (not being without law toward God, but under law toward Christ), that I might win those who are without law; to the weak I became as weak, that I might win the weak. I have become all things to all men, that I might by all means save some."
1 Corinthians 9:19-22

21. Champions league people also know that they must set a new agenda in the area of their calling.

Our world is changing technologically and geographically. Nations have been redefined in recent times. Some nations have even disappeared. There is no more Yugoslavia or Czechoslovakia. New nations have emerged. New geographical boundaries. The age of leadership has changed around the world. A good number of people who are emerging as Prime Ministers and Presidents in the western hemisphere are people in their forties.

Championship is not about age; it is about stage and impact.

Fearless faith requires that we must also see ourselves as people who should be a part of setting the agenda for changing our world.

22. They carry enough grace to enforce change

Remember, in this chapter, we looked at people in the champions league.

There are sports that have been around for hundreds of years; yet, in the past twenty to thirty years some people have shown and redefined that particular sport.

So, if I say basketball, your mind will go to Michael Jordan. If I say golf, your mind will go to Tiger Woods. There have been great players before them but when these two men appeared, they had enough grace to enforce change in the field of their sport.

It is my sincere prayer that a new generation will rise in the Body of Christ and they will enforce the kind of change that is beyond the ones we have read of; bigger than what Martin Luther the Reformer did, bigger than the revival of Sir Charles Finney or the expression of faith of Smith Wigglesworth.

THE FORCE OF CONFIDENCE

Paul's invitation to believers to appear before the throne of God to receive mercy and find grace was to encourage them not come with timidly but realise that they have been called and commissioned to be a people of confidence.

"Let us therefore come boldly to the throne of grace, that we may obtain mercy and find grace to help in time of need." Hebrews 4:16

We see this kind of confidence manifested by the lion. The lion is not afraid of any animal, it can take on prey several times bigger than it is.

"The wicked flee when no one pursues, but the righteous are bold as a lion." Proverbs 28:1

So, what is confidence?

> **All the people we respect in the world of Christianity have walked by godly confidence**

Confidence is full trust. It is resting in and believing in the power of something awesome. It is walking with audacity where others might dread. Confidence has a hint of trustworthiness. It is that ability to rely on a person or a thing, knowing that it cannot fail.

Confidence, as it relates to fearless faith is that belief in yourself as a result of the deposit made in you by God. This confidence will not let you cower in the face of battles, it makes you sure that the One who is with you is mightier than he who is in the world.

> *"You are of God, little children, and have overcome them, because He who is in you is greater than he who is in the world." 1 John 4:4*

Confidence is assurance. It is courage in the face of fire, certainty in a world of uncertainty, determination in a world of double-mindedness. It is being daring when others are dreading.

Confidence is to have the impudence to take on a seemingly impossible challenge, where others wonder "How can this be?"

Confidence is to be resolute, to be tenacious. In today's modern expression some would define confidence as having the nerve, the audacity.

So, fearless faith is an audacity of faith. Being audacious enough to believe that God can do anything as long as it is in consonance with His purpose, counsel and the advancement of His Word. As long as it promotes the well-being of His people.

> *"But as it is written: "Eye has not seen, nor ear heard, nor have entered into the heart of man the things which God has prepared for those who love Him.""* 1 Corinthians 2:9

As it relates to believers, confidence is a force because we mean the law or power to influence, to affect or control. This confidence is the strength of the spirit which helps the believer and gives that inner ability to win.

All the people we respect in the world of Christianity have walked by godly confidence.

Confidence is one of your most valuable assets because by it you will release greater blessings into your life. Confidence is not a destination; it is a journey you undertake.

Confidence is the ability of the successful to see even more success. It is the pointer to champions, the inner make-up of winners.

It is the component of men and women who have conquered their world.

Confidence is complete and total persuasion that the God who spun the universe into existence cannot lie. In fact, Paul calls it "full persuasion."

"For I am persuaded that neither death nor life, nor angels nor principalities nor powers, nor things present nor things to come, nor height nor depth, nor any other created thing, shall be able to separate us from the love of God which is in Christ Jesus our Lord." Romans 8:38-39

Confidence is a necessity because it gives us a firm belief, a trusting, a reliance in the ability of God to make certain what He promised.

Confidence is the inner conviction we have, so that in the face of any situation or matter we are able to see a way out where there seemed to be no way.

Confidence is the trust we have in a person or thing that they will come through for us. Confidence is the certain peace or certainty of the soul, the knowledge we have that we will achieve the dream and vision we already possess.

Confidence is the force that we express in the face of fear. It is courage and oldness.

> Confidence is complete and total persuasion that the God who spun the universe into existence cannot lie

Confidence causes us to undertake a task, no matter how challenging it may look.

Confidence is something every individual must acquire and develop in order to make progress in life.

The difference between the achiever and the loser can sometimes be confidence. It is seen in the animal kingdom and it is seen in the human kingdom.

There is a little animal somewhere in the southern part of Africa, known as the honey badger. It is the shape and size of a monkey but the honey badger is so peculiar. It takes on lions even though it is one tenth of their size. It grabs poisonous snakes, fights them and ends up eating them. My only conclusion is that the honey badger does these things because of confidence.

Confidence is like anti-bodies that spreads all over your body to fight the negative bacteria. Confidence infects and affects everything you do if you have it. It fuels your dream and gives you the boldness to face situations until your maximum potential manifests.

All the people we respect in the world of Christianity have walked by godly confidence

Confidence is like the electricity that allows you to release power and achieve the maximum potential of a piece of equipment. Imagine the air conditioner in a house or any piece of electrical equipment. They do not manifest their full capacity until the flow of power goes through them.

Confidence, when combined with competence gives you maximised performance.

Confidence is that voice in your spirit that tells you that you are able to do a thing when everyone around you says otherwise.

"Deep calls unto deep at the noise of Your waterfalls; All Your waves and billows have gone over me." Psalm 42:7

It is the stance of champions no matter what their age is. It is the kind of stance David had when he looked at an eleven-feet-nine-inch Goliath, who had been a man of war all his life. Goliath's spear looked like a weaver's beam and yet, David had confidence in his previous experience and testimony of conquest.

> "But David said to Saul, "Your servant used to keep his father's sheep, and when a lion or a bear came and took a lamb out of the flock, I went out after it and struck it, and delivered the lamb from its mouth; and when it arose against me, I caught it by its beard, and struck and killed it. Your servant has killed both lion and bear; and this uncircumcised Philistine will be like one of them, seeing he has defied the armies of the living God."" 1 Samuel 17:34-36

Confidence made an eighty-five-year-old Caleb ask for mountains when others were asking for their retirement benefits.

> "Now therefore, give me this mountain of which the Lord spoke in that day; for you heard in that day how the Anakim were there, and that the cities were great and fortified. It may be that the Lord will be with me, and I shall be able to drive them out as the Lord said."" Joshua 14:12

Confidence underwrote the attitude of Caleb and Joshua. Ten other men had a negative attitude about the Israelites possessing the land of Canaan, today we hardly remember the name of these ten men. We do not see their track record. As a matter of fact, they died in the wilderness. It is possible that Joshua and Caleb were no more gifted than those men, but the point of difference was their fearless faith.

Confidence is one of the greatest skills you can ever develop. Confidence is your bridge to success in your endeavours. It helps you and guards you against the forces that can come against your blessings.

When negativity comes, confidence makes you rise. When failure looks you in the face, confidence tells you that you can make it. When fear grips you, confidence strengthens you. When worry overwhelms you, confidence strengthens you. When you feel insecure in the face or presence of people who are more gifted, a certain degree of strength comes from the confidence you have in your own chosen field.

Confidence makes you unafraid to face negative forces and can turn them around, using them in a healthy manner to make progress.

"And we know that all things work together for good to

those who love God, to those who are the called according to His purpose." Romans 8:28

Confidence is your bridge to success in your endeavours

Only a highly confident man can make all things to work together for good. Anyone can quote scriptures but only those who walk the path of confidence can make it happen.

This attribute is great, but it cannot be bought. It can be developed, and we will see this further on. You will have to change your mindset in order to walk in confidence.

Romans 12 talks about renewing the mind. Many of us came into the faith with our self-esteem shattered and our confidence thrown away but now that we are in Christ, if we can allow the Word of God to flow richly into us, we can then develop the kind of confidence that can help us to overcome.

"Let the word of Christ dwell in you richly in all wisdom, teaching and admonishing one another in psalms and hymns and spiritual songs, singing with grace in your hearts to the Lord." Colossians 3:16

> **Confidence is a powerful current that influences everything in people's lives**

The process of walking in confidence starts with renewing the mind. Confidence is the defining difference between the common and the uncommon.

POWERFUL REASONS FOR THE PURSUIT OF CONFIDENCE

It was Samuel Johnson, the eighteenth-century English writer who said, *"Confidence is the first prerequisite to great undertakings. It is clearly related to our level of happiness.*[3]*"*

Why must you express or walk in confidence? Why is it a necessity for fearless faith?

Confidence is not a complicated trait to develop, yet many people do not walk in it. It does not require unusual intelligence or sophistication. It just requires a certain kind of resting in God. Why? Confidence takes you where many other giftings cannot take you. There are people who have unusual gifts and abilities, but they lack confidence and are therefore unable to progress.

So, confidence is greater than talent, looks and education. The absence of confidence makes you similar to an aeroplane full of passengers but without the fuel to command its take-off.

Confidence is an inborn trait placed in all men by God. Confidence is the hidden champion screaming for fulfilment. It is the inner champion waiting to emerge.

Confidence is that tool which helps us to embrace change very well. Change intimidates some people and for others, it is something to be feared but for the confident man, change is an opportunity to shine, to become the best.

Why must we walk in confidence?

Remember again we are talking about fearless faith and fearless faith cannot exist without confidence. An important factor to being successful in life and being happy, is your personal confidence. We need confidence because it is the factor between those who succeed and those who fail.

Confidence is a powerful current that influences everything in people's lives. It is shown in our conversation, in our personal lifestyle, in the atmosphere around us and even in the company we choose to keep. It is necessary in order to unlock the atmosphere of greatness that already exists in you.

Confidence propels your ability to achieve and makes you go forward. It is that trait in you that opens up unlimited abilities. Insecurities destroy your natural ability but confidence from God makes you see a way where there is no way and victory where there is imminent defeat.

If you doubt it, look at David as he confronted Goliath. With confidence, he answered King Saul.

"Your servant has killed both lion and bear; and this uncircumcised Philistine will be like one of them, seeing he has defied the armies of the living God."" 1 Samuel 17:36

We need confidence because we possess more potential on the inside to succeed than a tendency to fail. Confidence brings this out.

Many have failed in life because no one has ever told them how much they can achieve, what they can do. Rather, they have been told what they cannot do.

The possession of skills, wisdom and understanding will be limited by the absence of confidence.

What is the use of competence without confidence and what is the use of confidence without competence? A confident man who is incompetent will exhibit boldness but will be unable to deliver. A competent man who is not confident will have all the knowledge but be unable to use it.

Confidence propels your ability to achieve and makes you go forward

One of the most crippling effects on a person's confidence is their own self-doubt. God said He would be with the Children of Israel. Jehovah, the One who spoke the world into existence, Who by the word of His mouth can create or re-create was with them, yet they were still so full of self-doubt.

"But the men who had gone up with him said, "We are not able to go up against the people, for they are stronger than we."" Numbers 13:31

Confidence is needed because when you become content with where you are it will bring containment, and this can kill where you are going.

Confidence is the bridge between where you are now and where you want to go.

Why do we make this message important today?

> The difference between achieving children and non-achievers is sometimes the fact that somebody expressed

There are certain truths about it. We need a generation who are full of fearless faith to advance Christianity.

In recent times the kind of people who have looked boldly at the enemy and walked into dangerous zones have been people who full of dogma, who have rather wasted their own lives and other people's. This is almost to our shame.

We, as believers, have the truth because Jesus said we would know the truth and the truth would set us free. If we believe in the Gospel we preach and that it is the truth, then we need to walk in fearless faith. This will require the force of confidence.

Confidence is necessary for you to realise you are the best for the area God has chosen you to fulfil. Many do not have confidence in themselves. This is what we see in the life of Gideon when he was approached by the Angel of the Lord.

"Now the Angel of the Lord came and sat under the terebinth tree which was in Ophrah, which belonged to Joash the Abiezrite, while his son Gideon threshed wheat

in the winepress, in order to hide it from the Midianites. And the Angel of the Lord appeared to him, and said to him, "The Lord is with you, you mighty man of valor!""
Judges 6:11-12

Many people do not have another person who has expressed confidence in them. We all need someone to believe in us and push us beyond where we are comfortable.

The difference between achieving children and non-achievers is sometimes the fact that somebody expressed confidence in the ones who achieved. People can sense when we have shown true confidence in them. People always rise to the level of confidence we have shown in them. The confidence we express in a person positively changes their outlook on life.

Many who have ended up in jail have heard the constant prophecy from the mouths of those who were possibly their parents, guardians or leaders that they would never amount to anything good.

People are always seeking for someone to trust them, believe in them and help them to eventually become the best they will ever be. Like a magnet attracts metal, people attracted to a person who has confidence in them.

If you are still asking, "Why the force of confidence?"

Confidence is a language we use often even though we do not walk much in it. Through confidence we can achieve the things we never dreamt possible, as long as no one tells us it is impossible and even if they did, it would have no effect as you already know who you are in Christ.

Can you imagine if an ant went to a lesson to learn about how big a load it should carry? The ant would probably not attempt what it does! An ant will carry a load between thirty and fifty times its size, as long as it is not told it is impossible.

The bumble bee's wings aren't shaped aerodynamically strictly speaking; so theoretically it should not be able to fly. However, the bumble bee has never been told that because of the shape of its wings it cannot fly, so the bumble bee flies.

Confidence increases your personal level of achievement in life and helps you to believe in other people. It is your confidence in God and in yourself that helps you to have a healthy attitude towards others.

Once you are confident in what God can do through you and with you, your chances of wanting to put other people down become slim because you are not intimidated by, or feel inferior to others.

It is your confidence in God and in yourself that helps you to have a healthy attitude towards others

Those who do not have confidence in themselves find it hard to trust other people and even if they are given positive validation, they doubt it.

The difference between those who win in life and those who fail is always in their level of confidence. Confidence is necessary. When you begin to walk in it, it becomes contagious to those who are around you.

It will take confidence for one to chase a thousand and two to chase ten thousand, as the scriptures say.

"How could one chase a thousand, and two put ten thousand to flight, unless their Rock had sold them, and the Lord had surrendered them?" Deuteronomy 32:30

We see this in the example of Jonathan and his armour bearer. At a time when the Philistines had

When you are insecure, you are unable to handle blessing, both yours and that of others

an upper hand and Saul had not given the command to march forward to battle, the entire Israelite army gathered under trees. It was in the face of this that Jonathan and his armour bearer confronted the Philistines. Two men with minimal armour were so confident that Jehovah was able, having asked Him for assistance. They brought victory, humiliated the Philistines, took away the shame from the face of Israel and caused celebration in the camp of the people of God because of their confidence.

Confidence is a necessity. Achievement in life is more than a matter of working harder. It is a matter of behaving positively. Those who expect to succeed surely do so. Those who express confidence and expect to succeed enjoy success. Those who expect to fail fulfil their own prophecy.

Confidence produces history changers. That is what Jonathan and his armour-bearer did that day in battle. These kinds of men are often inventors, athletic stars. They rewrite history, introduce new languages to society and change long held beliefs.

Confidence is the only way to change your life. You cannot change your life unless you change your pattern of thinking. Your life today is built around your thoughts. If your thoughts are not succeeding, you will fulfil the prophecy of failure.

THE NEGATIVE THINGS WHICH CONFIDENCE DESTROYS

Walking in the grace of confidence is a master key for overcoming insecurity. When you are insecure, you are unable to handle blessing, both yours and that of others. The higher the challenges you face, the clearer your insecurities become.

Higher levels of leadership positions require more skills and a quicker and more effective decision-making capacity; whereas the person who is insecure lacks the kind of confidence they need.

You need confidence. Without it, you will compare yourself with other people all the time. You will become preoccupied with the status of other people, what they have achieved, how they have left you behind or have not carried you along, how you were once equals but now they have moved up in life. You consider their success as arrogance. You grumble and complain about why you are not on their level.

You judge others as being less worthy of the blessings than you. You do not feel good about your own accomplishments because you are always looking down on yourself. You need confidence because it is the only way to rise above comparison.

When you are insecure, you over compensate, you try to make up, you try to put on, you go hard on yourself. When a man is not confident, he schemes on how to get ahead, gain success and recognition and it is only a matter of scheming, not a matter of achievement. He begins to depend on personal qualities to advance himself. He is consumed with the pursuit of 'me and me and me.' He fights irrational battles to get what he thinks he deserves. He comes up with imaginary enemies who do not exist. He stoops to dishonesty and deception to get results.

Confidence in God and the gifts He placed in you and the ability you have raises you above this weakness. Insecurity can be daunting and limiting. When a person is insecure they become very competitive. They tend to outdo others, they need to receive attention, they tend to keep score in life. They do anything and everything just to win. A person who is insecure will be ungrateful, unteachable and jealous of other people's accolades and recognition.

> When you are insecure, you over compensate, you try to make up, you try to put on, you go hard on yourself

Insecure people tend to be full of pride. They are critical and judgemental of other people and of their blessings. They walk in lovelessness. They have a self-centred life. When confidence comes in, it helps a person to overcome.

Confident people are motivated by other people's achievements, they are not denigrated. They celebrate what others have done and use it as a motivation for their own achievements.

"Let nothing be done through selfish ambition or conceit, but in lowliness of mind let each esteem others better than himself." Philippians 2:3

When you have insecurities, you are an excessive people pleaser. You are driven to perform compulsively in order to gain people's approval. In

> **Insecurity is an enemy of confidence and fearless faith is an antidote for rising above it**

the end you risk burnout. Impure motives drive you to set unrealistic expectations.

Insecure people expect a lot of themselves because they are not secure in what they have done or what their gifts are. A man may have been given two-hundred members to watch over while another has two-thousand. If each man stays in his gift area, they will both be successful, according to their levels .The scripture says, "each according to his ability."

"And to one he gave five talents, to another two, and to another one, to each according to his own ability; and immediately he went on a journey." Matthew 25:15

When you are insecure you get into a performance mode, thinking, "the more I do, the more I will be appreciated." You have a hard time saying no because you do not want to disappoint people. You are unable to walk away from some invitations, for example, because you just have to be there and please everyone and, in the end, you please no one.

Insecurity makes you project yourself worth

more to others and overestimate your own importance. It is insecurity that makes a man overreact when his precise titles were not mentioned, maybe during an event or in introducing him.

When you are insecure, you experience self-pity. You get weary because you attempt to do too much for the wrong reasons; trying to please people is a destroyer.

When you find your confidence in God, it makes you secure in who you are and the gifts of God that are placed in you.

Insecurity can make you extremely hard on yourself. Self-condemnation is the behaviour of people who are insecure, because of a distorted reality and temptation to withdraw from responsibility. Insecurity makes you have a short-sighted perception of your own circumstances. You feel self-pity and loneliness as though you are the only one who endures hardship. You complain, you feel overwhelmed, you feel your own demise and insignificance.

Insecurity is an enemy of confidence and fearless faith is an antidote for rising above it.

It is important for you to realise beating yourself up for past mistakes, failures and hurts will never make you a confident person. Right the wrongs where it is possible and the ones you cannot correct, learn to live under the mercy of God. Stop beating yourself up and start thanking God for who you are. Everyone is beautiful for their situation.

"Beautiful for situation, the joy of the whole earth, is mount Zion, on the sides of the north, the city of the great King." Psalm 48:2 (KJV)

If you have insecurities, you always want to be in control. This is one end of the pendulum. On one hand some insecure people run away from responsibility. On another hand some want to take over and have control. In fact, they become control freaks. They are so afraid and want to take charge to protect their interests and monopolise situations. This is indicated by them feeling that other people are continually against them. They keep fighting with their co-workers and they become self-seeking and manipulative.

This chapter on confidence is in itself a whole mini-book. However, we leave it here because the focus is on the walk of people with fearless faith.

When a person is insecure, they are intimidated and deal with everyone from this standpoint. They scare people. They command others to come to order and line up. They cannot stand the success of other people. They feel that if people succeed then someone else must lose. They frequently blame others for their dilemmas and eventually suffer from a sense of wanting to prove something.

> **Stop beating yourself up and start thanking God for who you are**

Insecurity eats up fearless faith. You have to come to a sense of peace to know that you cannot control the world. You cannot control other people's joy. You cannot determine their destiny. Rather, be confident in whom God made you.

When you are insecure you tend to fear public failure. You avoid risk. You are not open to new relationships. You will not employ anyone stronger than you. You resist change.

Insecure people despise anyone who is different, whereas God created us to be different from other people. We are different, our gifts are unique. We are wonderfully made.

Do something you were afraid to do before and when you face criticism, do not fall apart

"I will praise You, for I am fearfully and wonderfully made; marvelous are Your works, and that my soul knows very well." Psalm 139:14

But the insecure do not see this. They cannot empower or affirm others. They would rather stay where they are: in charge. Sometimes an insecure person may be more gifted and could have attracted more by reason of their qualification and training, but they prefer to stay where they will be in charge. They talk all the time. They want positions and titles that make them feel important, even if it is just an empty title.

When you are going to the next level you must watch out for insecurity raising its ugly head. When you are expressing fearless faith, realise that any level you rise to is not yet final.

Be confident in what God is doing and be ready for a change. Do something for the first time, something that you have never done before. Change the way you have always done things. You will never discover your full potential if you do not do something beyond what you have done before.

So, break away from comfort zones, challenge yourself, stretch your faith, do not be afraid of failure, surround yourself with people who do not think that failure is final. Do something you were afraid to do before and when you face criticism, do not fall apart. The things you tried may have failed, the event organised may have failed but you are not a failure.

In 1976, my final year in Bible school, I organised a crusade. I expected a thousand people to come to the crusade ground. I was about to graduate. I set out chairs. I fasted and prayed for three days. But on the night of the crusade, eleven adults came along with six children. Loads of chairs but few people.

Did the Lord fail? Did my destiny fail? No! It was rather that the event I organised failed. I was a youth, I was inexperienced. No flyer was printed, publicity was poor, almost non-existent; and yet by some telepathy, I expected people to just know about the crusade and show up. I fasted and prayed but that was not enough. God will raise Lazarus, but He expected me to remove the stone.

If you are surrounded by critics, do not let them kill you. Your confidence can be destroyed in the atmosphere of criticism because of insecurity. Be confident in God. Do not let them condemn you.

"There is therefore now no condemnation to those who are in Christ Jesus, who do not walk according to the flesh, but according to the Spirit." Romans 8:1

It was Zig Ziglar who said, *"Don't be distracted by criticism. Remember: the only taste of success some people have is when they take a bite out of you.*[4]*"*

How many people have been told that they would not succeed, that they looked ugly? Clint Eastwood was told he would not succeed as an actor because he did not look handsome.

Make your confidence destroy the negatives.

Watch out when next you meet someone important. This is often the time when your insecurity shows. What do you do? We feel intimidated, our voices quiver, we make mistakes. The person may be important, but you are more important to God. Those people who look important to you always have their own similarities to you. They have a face, you have one. They have a head, you have one. They have bad days, you do too. They like the same things you like: good food, money, good clothes, success.

> **Make your confidence destroy the negatives**

When you meet successful people, celebrate them. Let people know how impressed you are with them and then that way, you find that you have shown that you are a likeable person.

Handle failure and watch out when your work fails.

Do not let your confidence go out of the window when you fail at the things you try. Confidence will empower you to overcome many attacks based on the failure of something you tried to do. Watch out when somebody close to you succeeds. Our insecurities often show up even more when someone we know succeeds.

Celebrate their blessings and wait for yours. Go the extra mile and boast of their success. That way you have taken away the chances of feeling bad. Watch out when your accomplishments are unrecognised. This is a major killer of confidence. Sometimes you wonder, "Have they not noticed what you did?" and then your insecurities show. If

> **The Bible speaks of overcomers and you are one of them**

you belong in a church, the chances are that when people were given the accolades and celebrated as 'Workers of the year', your name was not even on the list but you must rise above this and remember that you are good. God loves you.

Confidence is necessary to overcome your insecurities. A lack of confidence must lead you to find a life coach, someone who can help you become strong, who is not impressed by your failures or your previous successes. Identify the areas where you tend to be insecure. Confront them, overcome them. What you are unwilling to confront, you will never conquer. The soldiers of Israel were unwilling to confront Goliath and they could not conquer him. Rather, he seemed to grow by the day.

Talk to a trusted friend. Ask the person to tell you honestly where they see you expressing insecurity. Do not tell people your problem if they are unable to solve it.

This feedback should not come from people who are looking for a chance to take a bite at you.

Continue to build your confidence by doing things you have never done before. Let the champion in you continue to rise. Take on new territories. Study something new. Take an online course, study for a degree, learn a new subject. If you have to learn something new from your children, even if it's how to use your phone to do incredible things, go ahead. These are confidence builders. The Bible speaks of overcomers and you are one of them.

MAKING CONFIDENCE WORK FOR YOU

Fearless faith is not slang. It is not something you possess without using. You must use confidence to confront some things and fear is on of them. Why? Because God has not given you the spirit of fear. That is why we call it fearless faith.

There are too many things people tend to be afraid of. Confidence can help you overcome that kind of phobia.

1. The fear of success

Interestingly, many people are afraid to succeed because of the people who might criticise them. Yes, if you do not want to be criticised, laughed at, mocked and judged, do nothing and be nothing.

Use confidence to conquer the fear of failure. Many people are afraid to fail. The fear of failure will keep you from attempting the things you long to do.

Several years ago, I was on holiday and had to stay on a church's premises. The church had a school. It was an African setting. The kids made a makeshift high jump. Each kid came and jumped a particular level, but when it came to the turn of a one boy, whom we shall call Tom, he refused to jump. His friends came and jumped a second time but he never jumped. When his friends raised the bar to the next level, he complained, but they told him, "We have waited long enough for you." Tom was afraid of failing. He was afraid he might knock over the bar. He did not know that it is better to try and fail than to not try at all. The difference between Peter and the other eleven apostles was that Peter walked on water for a few seconds, while the other disciples never left the boat at all.

The difference between those who fail and those who succeed is that one person took a step and the other did nothing.

How do confident people really see fear? How do

they see failure? Confident people know that failure is not final, and success is not forever. Confident people see failure as an opportunity to improve, to become a better person; and if they ever succeed, they put that behind them and move on because today's

Use confidence to conquer the fear of failure

extraordinary is tomorrow's regular. They view failure as merely an opportunity to start all over again - and in a wiser way. They give themselves permission to fail so they can succeed.

This is very crucial. You must, somewhere in the inner recess of your heart, give yourself permission to fail so that when the failure comes you do not fall apart. Then move past the setbacks, the triumphs, the obstacles and the failures so that you can become great in life. You need to see failure as the price you pay in order to achieve the success you desire.

You should know that the fear of failure can stop you from going forward. Confront everything eating up your confidence. Confront fear, shame, guilt, humiliation, self-doubt, embarrassment and rise above them.

> **The person who attempts nothing has nothing, achieves nothing and becomes nothing**

The future is great, and the future is awesome.

2. The fear of rejection

Nobody wants to be turned down, put down, left out, kicked out, disliked and unwanted. We all want to be loved, accepted, respected, cared for, longed for and valued.

But, how do you overcome the fear of rejection? Overcome your fear of rejection by being confident in God, that He does not create junk. You are beautiful. You are absolutely wonderful. You are a Masterpiece. There are no two people who look like you, feel like you, talk like you. The colour of your hair may be similar to others but by just one hair on your head, you can be traced. Your DNA is extremely peculiar to you.

If you do not deal with your rejection, you will reject other people. The fear of rejection creates inaction. Confident people deal with rejection by learning to use it for their blessing, by learning to use it to shine.

3. The fear of taking a risk

Chris Bradford said, "He who is afraid to shake the dice will never throw six.[5]" One of the greatest defeats in life is never taking a risk. Some people have never done anything that requires risk-taking. The person who attempts nothing has nothing, achieves nothing and becomes nothing.

Many people have avoided risks, risky situations, pressures and criticisms. They have stayed in the comfort zones of life. Confidence is so necessary, because it helps you to realise that until you break away from the regular, you may never discover the unknown. To get out of a mess, to get out of the rut, you have to have guts, you have to make attempts, you have to do something you have never done before.

A person who lives an uncommon confident life will have to forge an uncommon path, but this can be blocked by your own thinking, disapproval, doubt and self-rejection.

Fear drives many people into poverty. Confidence drives you towards the path of a wealthy place.

"Thou hast caused men to ride over our heads; we went through fire and through water: but thou broughtest us out into a wealthy place." Psalm 66:12 (KJV)

Fear runs away from challenges. Confidence steers you towards the challenge because it is the challenge you conquer that gives you the testimony you desire. If there was no Goliath, there would be no David. Goliath did more for David than his seven brothers ever did.

You need what looks like opposition, an enemy, to build your confidence and make you win. If there was no mountain to climb, we would not have the testimony of great men who reached the summit.

4. The fear of poor health

So, how do you overcome the fear of poor health? Learn more about good health and keep yourself alive. Become confident. Resign today from the group of people who always say, "Until this happens, I cannot do that." Do not say, "Until this or that, until I have this, until I achieve that, until I have more time, until I make more money, until things change, until the conditions are favourable, until things settle down." Go out. Do something. Be confident.

If it has not happened, go and create it., Begin to do something real, something that shows your confidence TODAY. It only takes a small leap to break the gap between fear and confidence. When you take that step, the blessing will flow, the victory will flow, the testimony will flow.

> If there was no mountain to climb, we would not have the testimony of great men who reached the summit

Confidence is the bridge to taking your journey to the place God is taking you.

OPERATING UNDER THE FORCE OF CONFIDENCE

The knowledge about confidence is not enough. It is important to know how to walk under this grace. There are certain steps to take which will help and enhance, will change you from negativity to developing the kind of boldness required in the Holy Spirit.

The world makes room and respects anybody who walks in boldness, particularly if the source is the Holy Spirit.

Learn to reverse what people say when they speak negatively to you

"Now when they saw the boldness of Peter and John, and perceived that they were uneducated and untrained men, they marveled. And they realized that they had been with Jesus." Acts 4:13

So, develop your spirit man every day by reading and listening to messages that will increase your productivity and level of confidence. Have you noticed that when you prepare well on for matter that requires a response, your confidence level rises?

Have a personal commitment to growth. This will require sourcing for the right information all the time, which will help you with everything you face. The scriptures mention a church who, though they were ministered to by Paul, still went home to search if all they heard was true.

"Then the brethren immediately sent Paul and Silas away by night to Berea. When they arrived, they went into the synagogue of the Jews. These were more fair-minded than those in Thessalonica, in that they received the word with all readiness, and searched the Scriptures daily to find out whether these things were so." Acts 17:10-11

Thirdly put a high prospect to learning, particularly in the area where you want to excel and be confident. Learning is the beginning of success, the beginning of radical growth and radical blessing. It is the source of happiness and health.

Learning something new will help you in the transformation process, from being a timid person to a person capable of handling certain degrees of exposure, fame or limelight.

Learn to reverse what people say when they speak negatively to you. You need to develop a method for managing negative words spoken against you. When people say that you cannot do something, ask why not.

Eliminate all the limitations you have placed on yourself, all the negatives you have told yourself. Let the grace of God and the potential placed in you begin to replace these things. Look for someone who can help you develop a force of boldness and confidence. Every major achiever you know has someone who coaches them. Look for someone who will help you maximise your potential.

There are depths you cannot enter, heights you cannot reach if there is no one urging you to move on, someone showing you what the best way to do it is. One of the key reasons why many people fail is that they surround themselves with people who are not doing anything higher than them. Such people sometimes even celebrate them in the average level they operate in.

It is nearly impossible to maximise and maintain your confidence all by yourself. You need someone to push you. Those who have no one to stretch them can never become as good as they could have been. True wisdom is to learn from the winning wisdom, as well as the weakness of other people.

"Now all these things happened to them as examples, and they were written for our admonition, upon whom the ends of the ages have come." 1 Corinthians 10:11

How do you recognise confidence mentors? Such persons will care about your life's performance. They will be somebody who is interested in your dream and one way or the other, they will partner with it.

Confidence mentors will help you make adjustments in your personal life and create solutions that will help you overcome your challenges. A confidence mentor will help you evaluate your strengths, discover your capabilities and potential and push you in that direction.

One of the key reasons why many people fail is that they surround themselves with people who are not doing anything higher than them

A confidence mentor will be the voice of encouragement when you are discouraged. They will be the one who helps you move closer to your goal so that you can achieve all the dreams you carry in you.

THE TRIPOD OF CONFIDENCE

You need to recognise that the confidence that we are looking at here is not the one drawn from natural human boldness without God. The first leg of the tripod is "Confidence in God."

"But let him who glories glory in this, that he understands and knows Me, that I am the Lord, exercising lovingkindness, judgment, and righteousness in the earth. For in these I delight," says the Lord." Jeremiah 9:24

"If anyone speaks, let him speak as the oracles of God. If anyone ministers, let him do it as with the ability which

Express strong faith and confidence in what God can do in your and through you

God supplies, that in all things God may be glorified through Jesus Christ, to whom belong the glory and the dominion forever and ever. Amen." 1 Peter 4:11

Your roots start with God. Make Him the partner in your life and your confidence level will rise.

Secondly you must have confidence in yourself. You will succeed if you believe in the fact that abilities have been deposited in you.

Thirdly you must show confidence in others.

Let us take these three together. If you do not believe in what God can do in you and through you, you will have difficulty believing in other people.

The foundation of confidence is based on belief. If there is no belief, there cannot be real confidence. I want you to imagine yourself entering public transport, be it a bus, a train or a plane. You confidently sit on the seat provided with the confidence that the people who provided this means of transportation would not install a seat that could not hold your weight.

Many expect you to fail so, if you must move up the ladder, you must realise that you too must not expect yourself to fail.

Take things one by one and do not expect yourself to fail. Move to the next level where you wish you could succeed. Take it further and begin to pray that you will succeed. Move on and know that you can succeed. Then, believe you can succeed and finally expect and have confidence that you will succeed.

Build your confidence level because it is easier to believe bad things than it is to believe good ones.

Express strong faith and confidence in what God can do in your and through you.

"But by the grace of God I am what I am, and His grace toward me was not in vain; but I laboured more abundantly than they all, yet not I, but the grace of God which was with me." 1 Corinthians 15:10

The only thing that stands between a man and what he wants from life is often the will to try it and have the faith to believe that it is possible.

So, if we must have fearless faith, we must have this kind of confidence. In the words of Richard

Devos, "Refuse to listen to that little voice telling you that you cannot make any difference, that you are just nothing in this world."

Contrary to this statement, 1 John 4:4 says, *"You are of God, little children, and have overcome them, because He who is in you is greater than he who is in the world."*

So, never sell yourself short. When you start believing that you are worth millions of dollars, people will treat you that way. See yourself as God sees you. Stop judging yourself by your skin colour, height, gender or the place of your abode. You are many times bigger than all of these barometers by which people measure life.

Change begins to manifest when you believe you can achieve the impossible and when you begin to change the way you think.

"Finally, brethren, whatever things are true, whatever things are noble, whatever things are just, whatever things are pure, whatever things are lovely, whatever things are of good report, if there is any virtue and if there is anything praiseworthy—meditate on these things." Philippians 4:8

CONFIDENT THINKING

Your thinking must change in order for you to experience a new level of blessing and success. True success is never measured by the degrees you have or the family you come from. It is measured by the size of your thoughts. Everything

> **Stop judging yourself by your skin colour, height, gender or the place of your abode**

God does starts with a thought. Everything all humans do starts with a thought. From a little thing such as dressing up in the morning, to creating nuclear plants. Everything starts with a thought.

Whatever you will become in life is already pre-determined by the size of your thoughts. How big you think determines the size of your dreams and achievements.

> *"For as he thinks in his heart, so is he. "Eat and drink!" he says to you, but his heart is not with you." Proverbs 23:7*

I know there has been a lot of writing on the power of thoughts, but I must bring your attention to the fact that where you are today is the product of your thoughts. What you have become is a product of your thoughts. Picking up this book was because a thought went through your mind.

> Every time something positive comes up, your mind will reject it as being too good because your thoughts are negative

Thomas Stanley said, *"Before you can become a millionaire you must learn to think like one."*

When you change your thinking, you will change how you view yourself. When you have self-doubt, negativity and self-defeating thoughts, you will walk according to your thinking. Of all the muscles in our life, the most powerful is the brain, but interestingly enough, when you go into a gym, that is not the muscle people develop.

There are men with muscles so hard and strong, chests as wide as Australia, and yet, they have never picked up a book to stretch their thinking.

The thought muscle can be elasticated to accommodate and prepare us for a life of confidence. Check your thinking, because it is controlling your journey and your destination. Where you are now is as a result of what has gone through your mind. If you do not mind your mind, no one will mind you.

Where you are now is a result of what has gone through your mind. Whatever you think of all day is what you will become the rest of your days. How big you think is revealed in your level of confidence. If you cannot see yourself achieve, accomplish or become, it will never truly happen.

Thinking differently, thinking bigger thoughts opens up a world of possibilities.

"Jesus said to him, "If you can believe, all things are possible to him who believes."" Mark 9:23

However, if you have negative thoughts in your mind it will filter through your life, even if you speak differently. Every time something positive comes up, your mind will reject it as being too good because your thoughts are negative.

Therefore, if your dreams are huge, if your desire of the future is to succeed and be happy, you need to begin the development of thoughts that you and God can make happen.

"Through God we will do valiantly, for it is He who shall tread down our enemies." Psalm 60:12

"Your people shall be volunteers in the day of Your power; in the beauties of holiness, from the womb of the morning, you have the dew of Your youth." Psalm 110:3

When you start to think and dream this way, everything around you will begin to change. When little people come and want to drag you back to yesterday, think bigger. When non-achievers come to criticise you, think bigger. When discouragers come to tell you it cannot be done, it has never been done, or it will not be done, think bigger. When all the odds seem against you, think bigger.

Your emotional confidence cannot become any stronger than your mind. It is not possible. Your mind cannot rise above the level of its thoughts. The level of confidence you express, the state of your mind, is in direct proportion to the strength of your mind.

Certain things are involved in the force of confidence: a man's thoughts, his emotions and then his actions. They must all see possibilities before they come to pass. The greater the challenge you desire to achieve and to overcome, the greater your mental and emotional preparation.

"Rejoice in the Lord always. Again I will say, rejoice! Let your gentleness be known to all men. The Lord is at hand. Be anxious for nothing, but in everything by prayer and

supplication, with thanksgiving, let your requests be made known to God; and the peace of God, which surpasses all understanding, will guard your hearts and minds through Christ Jesus." Philippians 4:4-7

When all the odds seem against you, think bigger

It must start with your thinking. Once that changes, your emotional feelings change. Refuse to be bogged down with discouragement, frustration, limitation and depression. The way you feel is tied to the way you believe. Start to see God making a way for you where there seems to be no way.

"Behold, I will do a new thing, now it shall spring forth; shall you not know it? I will even make a road in the wilderness and rivers in the desert. The beast of the field will honor Me, the jackals and the ostriches, because I give waters in the wilderness and rivers in the desert, to give drink to My people, My chosen." Isaiah 43:19-20

Change your feeling and your actions and behaviour will change. Negative thoughts will cross your mind, but you have the power to not dwell on them. Get rid of every bad thought and attitude.

The most powerful stopper of the force of confidence is a negative attitude. Attitude is a deep

-seated chosen belief, either positive or negative, that sets corresponding behaviour (generally resulting in self-fulfilling prophecies) in motion.

> When you walk under the influence of a poor attitude, you turn people off, people will avoid you

Attitude is that inward belief, that inward feeling. In life, it is your attitude, not aptitude that determines your altitude. Men do not rise only because of what they know. The Christian's rise comes from attitude. That is why you will find a man who probably struggled to finish the equivalent of secondary school hiring MBAs and PHDs. Academics is good, but if the attitude is wrong, it will not give a man the wings to fly.

The actions you carry out are ultimately determined by the attitude you have. When the force of confidence increases in you, your attitude will become positive. It will show on the outside. It will become everything to you. When you face good or bad situations your confidence in God will not stop. Why? Because you have the right attitude.

Therefore, to achieve a positive attitude surround yourself with people who are confident, strong and positive. With this, you will see a world of opportunity, happiness and blessing.

Protect your attitude, just as you protect your briefcase or money. Protect it from negative people. Surround yourself with confidence boosters, people who tell you it can be done, it will be done.

When you walk under the influence of a poor attitude, you turn people off, people will avoid you. Even those who have a negative attitude want someone who is positive. Isn't that interesting? If you walk with a negative attitude, you will experience one failure after another. Your confidence level will be at the lowest.

Attitude is powerful. It helps you to bring balance to your life irrespective of how people behave towards you. If your attitude is poor, when people do not like you, your confidence will be shaken; when people reject you, your confidence will be shaken; when people talk about you negatively, it will rattle you because you have not decided to develop a good positive attitude towards yourself and life. These are a necessity if you must develop fearless faith.

DRAWING THE SWORD OF UNCOMMON CONFIDENCE

In this chapter, we have taken quite a bit of time to share on the power of confidence. Let us look at the subject again, on a higher level.

A higher dimension of confidence is possible. The scripture is full of statements that challenge us to excel, to do the unusual.

> *"But those who wait on the Lord shall renew their strength; they shall mount up with wings like eagles, they shall run and not be weary, they shall walk and not faint." Isaiah 40:31*

> *"Now this is the confidence that we have in Him, that if we ask anything according to His will, He hears us." 1 John 5:14*

> *"Delight yourself also in the Lord, and He shall give you the desires of your heart." Psalm 37:4*

> *"But He said, "The things which are impossible with men are possible with God."" Luke 18:27*

In this section we want to discuss how to have a higher dimension confidence. It is very important, in the journey of life, that we do not only walk in confidence, but operate in a higher dimension of it. This way, we will be able to access all that God has for us, achieve our own dreams, fulfil our vision and reach our destiny in the end.

> **The scripture is full of statements that challenge us to excel, to do the unusual**

"I have fought the good fight, I have finished the race, I have kept the faith." 2 Timothy 4:7

An uncommon confidence is about the how to - what to do precisely to move to a higher level of confidence. It has to do with how to get out of the box of the regular, or from the norm to a level of the uncommon. For this to happen it may have to mean getting ready to move into a scenario, a level you have never seen any of your peers walk into.

How do you do this?

1. You must change your self-portrait so you can change your performance

People will have an image and portrait they have painted of you. Do not adopt it if it does not rest well with uncommon confidence.

2. Do not allow other people to create an image of failure in you or destroy your image of success

The yardstick people often use, which leads to

God's portrait of you is awesome, it is so great and it is the best yardstick

the opinions they hold, is oftentimes based on faulty information or, in these days of social media, poor information can also sour the impressions others have of you.

3. Reject the labels people have given you because their labels can cripple you OR limit your confidence and potential in God

This happened to Jabez and it came from none other than his mother, until he shook it off.

"Now Jabez was more honorable than his brothers, and his mother called his name Jabez, saying, "Because I bore him in pain." And Jabez called on the God of Israel saying, "Oh, that You would bless me indeed, and enlarge my territory, that Your hand would be with me, and that You would keep me from evil, that I may not cause pain!" So God granted him what he requested." 1 Chronicles 4:9-10

Some people will describe you by your past failures, challenges, or the negative home you came from but you are not your past, you are not their opinion, you are whom God says you are.

4. You are much better than people have said you are

You are even better than what you have said you are. Everyone's perspective of you and your own perspective of yourself is often based on certain conclusions.

God's portrait of you is awesome, it is so great and it is the best yardstick.

"What is man that You are mindful of him, and the son of man that You visit him? For You have made him a little lower than the angels, and You have crowned him with glory and honor." Psalm 8:4-5

5. Your personal level of confidence is determined by your self-talk, self-esteem and self-image

Today the Church is under attack. Our faith is criticised. Our beliefs are criticised. Our people are ostracised. Satan is mesmerizing the world. That is why fearless faith is vital.

6. How you see yourself determines the level of success you will achieve in life

The Bible says to go and learn from the ant.

"Go to the ant, you sluggard! Consider her ways and be wise," Proverbs 6:6

The ant sees itself as capable of carrying loads thirty times its normal weight. It has never felt stressed. It has no leader or commander and yet it carries out its tasks.

7. Your positive self-image is a major key to your future success

Again, we have quoted Psalm 8:4-5. This is God's view of you. Let it radically reshape your mind. One of the ways to do this is to find scriptures that paint the exact picture of how God sees you and read them consistently to yourself (Psalm 139; Psalm 8).

8. You are motivated to become what you picture yourself to be

You will only rise to the image of the picture you see of yourself.

9. Your poor self-esteem creates an invisible barrier which prevents you from achieving your full potential and sends an invisible message of rejection to any blessing greater than the yardstick, the levels you have drawn.

In the Book of Zechariah, God sends a message to a young man, a surveyor, who takes the plumb line and measures the length and breadth of Jerusalem. For him, that is how big the city could be. God sends a message to him to say, "The city I am about to build is bigger than what you have imagined."

> **You will only rise to the image of the picture you see of yourself**

I have been to Jerusalem several times. Old Jerusalem with its walls is now like a tiny ward inside the bigger Jerusalem, probably no bigger than ten per cent of what it is now. Jerusalem has spread so much that there is hardly a gap between it and adjacent cities.

10. It is impossible to out-perform your inner self-image

11. A godly self-image helps you to see goals that reflect your true potential

12. You must remember that images are created by your own thoughts

If I begin to describe the beautiful sandy shores of Kingston, Jamaica or the white sands of Mauritius, your mind immediately can see the picture.

Start seeing yourself through the image of success

"For as he thinks in his heart, so is he. "Eat and drink!" he says to you, but his heart is not with you." Proverbs 23:7

At the same time, if I describe the image of a war-torn city where people are forced to feed on leftover food from the dustbins, eating rotten food just to survive, wearing clothes that are dirty because there is no water; people who have not washed in six months, with hair full of lice, you can immediately see the picture as well.

13. For you to change the wrong image, you have to change the wrong thoughts you think of yourself

14. Your thoughts are a product of the words you hear, your own self-talk in particular

That is why you need to avoid every picture, every word, every environment, every person who paints anything contrary to the things you believe in.

Even television now demands that we be selective about what we watch.

15. You must control the place from which you get your information

To do this, you need to delete everything that is not in agreement with fearless faith, cancelling every handwriting that does not agree with where you are going.

"having wiped out the handwriting of requirements that was against us, which was contrary to us. And He has taken it out of the way, having nailed it to the cross." Colossians 2:14

16. Create a new image of success, stop looking at yourself through the glass of failure

Start seeing yourself through the image of success.

17. See a confident champion who is full of potential, enthusiasm, personality, a promised future, success on all sides, good things happening to you, people loving you and people coming to help you

18. Love yourself as God loves you

Many times, out of false humility, we will say, "Jesus, Others, then Yourself...JOY." However, I am personally convinced this contradicts the teaching of Jesus. Jesus Himself said, "Love your neighbour as yourself." In other words, the degree of love you can give your neighbour is determined by the quality of love you have for yourself.

19. You need to overcome a poor self-image because it is the root of anxiety, depression, fear, alcohol problems, drug abuse, underachievement, dysfunctional lives, emotional immaturity etc.

20. The absence of self-love can ALSO result in all self-rejection, self-mutilation, self-punishment, over-indulgence in certain negative things, eating disorders, prostitution, self-abuse etc.

21. You must accept yourself before you can really like anyone else

Today as we speak about fearless faith and having confidence, you need to realise that before you can accept the fact that you deserve to succeed and be happy, it must first start with the acceptance of who God made you to be.

"So God created man in His own image; in the image of God He created him; male and female He created them." Genesis 1:27

22. The image of God is not the image of failure

Always remember He created you, He created you in His image and when the image was dented at the fall in the Garden, He sent the last Adam, His Son, to redeem you and then you became born-again into the family of God.

> The degree of love you can give your neighbour is determined by the quality of love you have for yourself

23. Failure to accept the fact that you are created for success will make you resign to playing the role of a loser and victim

It will lead to self-hatred and self-hatred destroys confidence.

24. Discover your true value

Jesus said, "And what shall a man give in exchange for his soul?" The previous verse says, "What shall it profit a man if he gained the whole world and loses his soul."

This scripture suggests that the planet's entire real estate is not comparable in value to one soul in the sight of God. You are valuable.

"I will praise You, for I am fearfully and wonderfully

> **If you are struggling to accept compliments, there are inner issues you need to deal with**

made; marvelous are Your works, and that my soul knows very well." Psalm 139:14

25. Change what you think of the value God has placed on you

Realise that you have something to contribute to the world that no one else can. You are more valuable than diamonds or any precious stone - ever.

26. Stop trying to be somebody else

Be who God said you would be. If God wanted you to be someone else, He would not have created you to have a different face. You are unique. No one looks like you because God intended you to remain a masterpiece, an original.

27. You can make a difference and your difference can make you

Allow your difference to define you, not confine you. My voice is unique because it was meant to define me and not confine me. My shape, image, colour, gender is unique because it was meant to define me. It was meant to show who I am and not limit and confine me.

28. Begin the journey today into daily success

Consider the fact that there is no rough day, bad day or evil day planned by God. Every day was ordained to be a success as long as you draw your motivation from His Word.

"This Book of the Law shall not depart from your mouth, but you shall meditate in it day and night, that you may observe to do according to all that is written in it. For then you will make your way prosperous, and then you will have good success." Joshua 1:8

"Blessed be the Lord, Who daily loads us with benefits, the God of our salvation! Selah" Psalm 68:19

29. Accept compliments when people pay them to you

If you are struggling to accept compliments, there are inner issues you need to deal with.

30. The appreciation people show you are vitamins for strengthening your confidence, self-esteem and self-image

31. Disconnect from wrong people

The people you are relating to are a mirror of how you think you deserve to be treated. Do not surround yourself with people who are struggling to even appreciate the success you have seen.

Rather, surround yourself with people who feel that you can do more, can achieve more and carry grace.

32. If you do not embrace healthy positive challenging relationships, you will naturally move towards destructive ones

How many young men and women who had incredible potential have been destroyed because of false love, or wrong associations with people who have drawn them into all kinds of lifestyles that ended up being ruinous?

33. Fall in love with whom God made you to be

Recognise your need to be treated nicely. Do not accept junk anywhere you go. The reason you go to high level restaurants is for them to celebrate you and create the atmosphere that makes you feel needed, wanted and appreciated.

When you go to these restaurants, the very food they serve may even be the same as those used by a cheaper restaurant as chicken is chicken. However, whether it is a small eatery or a high-end restaurant, what we buy is ambience, service and the celebration of the customer.

34. Stop asking yourself "what did I do wrong?"

Some people always look at life from the angle of the wrong. Stop

Recognise your need to be treated nicely

playing the blame game – focusing on the people who have abused you. Start talking about the things you have overcome and how you have come out strong, instead of the things that momentarily took you down.

35. Do not be afraid to disconnect from any relationship that is destroying your joy and confidence in God

Everyone you meet is either a door, a bridge or a wall. Those who are a wall will stop you. Bridges will take you to the next level.

36. Develop the language of a champion

Champions know the secret of a positive confession. Remember we are challenging people into fearless faith. To exercise and experience fearless faith will require a movement away from the regular.

Political correctness is another way to describe trying to mesh and fit into how people want things.

> It is what you say to yourself after they stop talking that determines how you feel

37. Most of your emotion is determined by what you say to yourself, so, say the right things

"But his delight is in the law of the Lord, and in His law he meditates day and night." Psalm 1:2

38. A positive personality plus a positive appreciation of who you are will result in a positive confession

Once you can see that you are blessed, you have a life worth living, your confession will change.

39. How you view yourself determines your inner dialogue

So, improve your self-image and self-esteem and you will change your self-talk.

40. What others say is not what really makes you feel bad

It is what you say to yourself after they stop talking that determines how you feel.

"Death and life are in the power of the tongue, and those who love it will eat its fruit." Proverbs 18:21

People will never be stopped from having an opinion of you. You are the one who can create firewalls that stop their negative talk, opinions etc. from reaching you.

41. Transform your "I AM" confessions

Many times, people grow up with very negative I AMs. Firstly, when you look into the scriptures we see that every I AM Jesus said was positive. "I am the door, the way, the truth, the life, the Shepherd."

People love to say "I am" but they attach something that is negative to it. Things like "I am worthless, I am fat, I am poor, I am ugly, I am a failure, I am stupid, I am a misery, I am bad, I am a mistake, I am unlovable."

You need to change all this to "I am worthy of success as a child of God, I am blessed and highly favoured, I am a happy person, I am loved, accepted and valued, I am brilliant and beautiful, I am smart enough to do anything I want, I can do all things through Christ, I am smart enough to figure out solutions to problems, God has given me a beautiful mind, I am good enough through Christ, there is no more condemnation for me."

"There is therefore now no condemnation to those who are in Christ Jesus, who do not walk according to the flesh, but according to the Spirit." Romans 8:1

YOUR CONFIDENCE IS SHOWING

There is a physical manifestation of confidence. People will see it and know it is there. It starts with how you dress. You need to dress the way you want to be addressed. When you dress for success, you present an appearance of confidence, success, wisdom and excellence.

> *"So it was, when the king's command and decree were heard, and when many young women were gathered at Shushan the citadel, under the custody of Hegai, that Esther also was taken to the king's palace, into the care of Hegai the custodian of the women. Now the young woman pleased him, and she obtained his favor; so he readily gave beauty preparations to her, besides her allowance. Then seven choice maidservants were provided for her from the king's palace, and he moved her and her maidservants to the best place in the house of the women." Esther 2:8-9*

Esther was raised in the slave quarters with a pre-fixed kind of clothing to wear and no perfume or adornment. However, in order to woo the king, she needed to change and have an appearance of success. The king was accustomed to a certain kind of presentation and he would not lower his standard for anyone.

The spirituality of Esther's uncle did not stop him from seeing the need to be properly dressed. If you do not put a nice cover on your body, people will receive you as a bad book. There is a lot of debate

You need to dress the way you want to be addressed

as to what Christian dressing is and what is not. It is very difficult to put a tag on a particular style and call it Christian dressing. However, in the world in which we live, where looks and appearances are used to judge, confidence also manifests in the way people dress themselves.

Remember our subject as we come to a close of this chapter is "uncommon confidence."

Your physical appearance needs to be a testimony. Adam loved what he saw in Eve. Isaac fell in love with his bride from day one. There must be an attraction. Esther attracted the king of a whole empire. Dressing for success improves your performance and how you are perceived.

THE FINAL PREPARATIONS

So, are you ready to walk out in fearless faith and show your confidence? Let us put a finishing touch to how you must prepare and carry yourself with confidence.

1. Champions are made in the process of their preparations

You must not neglect the path of preparation

"But sanctify the Lord God in your hearts, and always be ready to give a defense to everyone who asks you a reason for the hope that is in you, with meekness and fear;" 1 Peter 3:15

2. Preparing yourself today, you position yourself for an excellent chance for achieving your desired outcome in life

You must not neglect the path of preparation.

3. Preparation is so key to confidence

This has to do with your immediate preparation and future one. Future preparations have to do with years of getting ready to become the best that you can be.

Imagine a person who wants to be the president of a nation. He cannot wake up one day and scream, "Eureka! I found it. I want to be the president." There has to be years of getting ready, a building up one's confidence to take on such a daunting position.

Then, there is daily preparation. That aspect where you watch daily and ensure that you are building your confidence level and expressing fearless faith.

> *"Blessed is the man who listens to me, watching daily at my gates, waiting at the posts of my doors."* Proverbs 8:34

4. Your continued pursuit of mental, emotional and spiritual goals is a pointer to the preparation for winning

5. Champions are not just born, they are made in the process of the preparation

Great weapons of war do not become the best at the time of their use. It starts from when they are being prepared. One of the programs I love to watch is how swords, knives and spears are made. It is a competition called "Forged in Fire" and the man who makes the best item eventually wins $10,000.

It is not just the weapon that is made, it is the preparation. Oftentimes the one who wins eventually is not the one that looks the most beautiful, but the one that can cut, kill, stand the test without breaking, bending etc.

6. Champions do not become champions in the ring of operation, but in their daily routine of preparation

7. Preparation is the difference between winning and losing

You do not tune your instrument after the concert. A man who will play his guitar well must tune it first. A man who will use a weapon well cannot figure out how to do so in the face of battle, he must train first.

8. Getting ready is the secret of success

9. Those who take the time to prepare make themselves ready for perfection

Preparation is 95% of winning. Proper Preparation Prevents Poor Performance.

10. Enrich your potential by becoming an expert in your chosen field through intense preparation

"Being confident of this very thing, that He who has begun a good work in you will complete it until the day of Jesus Christ." Philippians 1:6

Nothing builds confidence like adequate preparation.

11. Your confidence will multiply because of increased information

Whenever I go to speak, confidence levels rise when I know that the subject I am about to share on is the one I have prepared a lot about.

> **You do not tune your instrument after the concert**

12. When you prepare very well, your confidence towards your dream and goal will increase

Confidence helps people to be able to listen to your thoughts and perspective because you will flow very well. People will put more confidence in you and your abilities. It will make you gain respect and followership of others. You will become an asset anywhere you go. Your knowledge of other subjects will instantly multiply.

"Be diligent to present yourself approved to God, a worker who does not need to be ashamed, rightly dividing the word of truth." 2 Timothy 2:15

13. Invest in your most valuable asset, your mind

"Therefore you are inexcusable, O man, whoever you are who judge, for in whatever you judge another you

> **Start painting a picture of the future and a higher level of confidence will rise in you**

condemn yourself; for you who judge practice the same things. But we know that the judgment of God is according to truth against those who practice such things." Romans 2:1-2

The arena of winning or losing is the mind. Once your mind is working in consonance with what you want to do, you are able to stand and speak with confidence.

14. Become a lifelong student

The more you learn the more you earn and the less you yearn in the latter part of your life. This must be the reason why God told Joshua that the recipe for success, particularly when you have to occupy a place previously occupied by a person like Moses, would be constant meditation in the truth that is able to elasticate your mind.

> "This Book of the Law shall not depart from your mouth, but you shall meditate in it day and night, that you may observe to do according to all that is written in it. For then you will make your way prosperous, and then you will have good success." Joshua 1:8

The same formula for success was given to Timothy by Paul.

"Till I come, give attention to reading, to exhortation, to doctrine." 1 Timothy 4:13

To prepare, you may have to learn to turn your car into a school on wheels. Instead of perpetually complaining about the traffic jam, use the time to expose yourself to every seminar that can help you in your chosen field. material is now available on USBs, CDs and can be played in your car.

15. Preparing today gives you confidence for tomorrow

Start painting a picture of the future and a higher level of confidence will rise in you.

16. It is necessary for you to pursue the dreams in your spirit

You must go the full length of the journey from dream to goals then to a plan, and from a plan to an action and from action to a realisation.

17. High dimension confidence requires that you do not die with your dream but fulfil it

Your dream must not expire until it becomes a reality.

18. You must believe that you can achieve these dreams and let the dreams give your life

direction and confidence

19. You need to commit yourself to a future you have not even seen yet

If you dream of it as a possibility, then it will become a reality.

"While we do not look at the things which are seen, but at the things which are not seen. For the things which are seen are temporary, but the things which are not seen are eternal." 2 Corinthians 4:18

STAY IN THE GAME

As we wrap up our study on confidence as a believer's stance, you must have the understanding that your capacity to stand, stay and succeed will be tested.

Your confidence level will show during some tests. What do you do when even those you believe in, who are supposed to help you, turn their backs on you?

1. You must determine when never to quit on yourself

This staying power increases your confidence. Make up your mind that even if others quit on you, you will not quit.

You must realise that success favours people who are confident because they never give up.

> "The end of a thing is better than its beginning; the patient in spirit is better than the proud in spirit."
> Ecclesiastes 7:8

Make up your mind that even if others quit on you, you will not quit

We said it earlier that those who quit never win and the ones who win never quit.

A majority of people in life are quitters, but you must not be with the majority. Confidence is boosted by the desire to stay in the game to the end and to learn. So, persistence, perseverance and determination are necessary for reaching your goal. If the turtle and the snail made it to the Ark of Noah, you too can make it to your desired goal.

If you have to adapt, then you should. The lack of adaptation makes the great and the small to disappear. Dinosaurs are no longer here because they would not adapt. Cockroaches made it because they chose to adapt.

2. You have also a need for patience

> "For you have need of endurance, so that after you have done the will of God, you may receive the promise"
> Hebrews 10:36

Do they not say that the patient dog gets the best bone? But I think he gets much better than that.

> **Open yourself to learning and growing, even if you have to learn from someone younger or subordinate, as long as you learn**

Move from patience to persistence

"Therefore take up the whole armor of God, that you may be able to withstand in the evil day, and having done all, to stand." Ephesians 6:13

Move from persistence to perseverance

Endure until what was once your breaking point becomes your starting point. Be so determined that quitting is not in your dictionary.

"Looking unto Jesus, the author and finisher of our faith, who for the joy that was set before Him endured the cross, despising the shame, and has sat down at the right hand of the throne of God." Hebrews 12:2

3. Remember, it is not only thoughts that must change, your language must now change.

You must speak like a confident person.

"Death and life are in the power of the tongue, and those who love it will eat its fruit." Proverbs 18:21

Build a language full of confident words and statements. Be a "can do" person.

"I can do all things through Christ who strengthens me."
Philippians 4:13

To do this, you must replace these phrases and words: "I cannot, impossible, too hard, I will try, I do not think, if, if only, I doubt it, maybe, I do not believe it, I do not have time, I am stressed, I am afraid."

You need to replace the above with "can do" words like, "I can, it is possible, it is too easy, I will do it, I know, I will, next time, I expect the best, I do believe, I will make the time, I am motivated, it will be all right." These are the expressions of the fearless.

4. Resign from the group of those who blame someone or something else for their future and their failure

5. Do not act like you know everything

Open yourself to learning and growing, even if you have to learn from someone younger or subordinate, as long as you learn.

If you do not know something, open yourself up to learning about it and communicate your lack of knowledge in that area with confidence, so that it

Be fearless, be faith-full is not something that taunts you and makes you feel ashamed.

Do not be afraid to ask. My mother used to say, "the one who asks for directions never misses the road."

"So I say to you, ask, and it will be given to you; seek, and you will find; knock, and it will be opened to you." Luke 11:9

Be fearless, be faith-full. That way, you will make your confidence contagious.

---

[3] https://www.brainyquote.com/quotes/samuel_johnson_122529

[4] https://quotefancy.com/quote/63455/Zig-Ziglar-Don-t-be-distracted-by-criticism-Remember-the-only-taste-of-success-some

[5] https://www.goodreads.com/quotes/1214474-he-who-is-afraid-to-shake-the-dice-will-never

THE FEARLESS

Wikipedia describes fear as "a feeling induced by perceived danger or threat that occurs in certain types of organisms, which causes a change in metabolic and organ functions and ultimately a change in behaviour, such as fleeing, hiding, or freezing from perceived traumatic events.[6]"

Fear is possibly one of the most universal emotions. One of the things tested when a baby is born is its capacity to show shock. This gives the medical doctor the sense that the baby is emotionally strong and capable of expressing emotion at the sight of danger, fear etc.

This book is about fearless faith. Let us face it, there is fear in the world, all kinds of fear. We all go

The levels of fear in individuals is dependent on what they have experienced in life through it from childhood to the grave: fear of failure, fear of heights, fear of poverty and lack and for some, fear of abundance; fear of animals; all kinds of animals from the wild to even the tamed; fear of flying, fear of perishing, fear of old age, fear of rejection. People fear the future. If they want or even if they do not want to, someone will scare them about something in the future. Fear of insects and bugs. The fear of being alone. The fear of the dark, of the dead. The fear of the sea or water in general, particularly when it seems to be deep.

The Bible talks of the fear of man. Fear of diseases. The levels of fear in individuals is dependent on what they have experienced in life. Some people have been in the atmosphere where there was an accident. Therefore, you can trace their fear and shock to the possibilities of some kind of collision or danger. Fear can come through abnormal attitudes from those who were around you and make you lose confidence.

Receiving shocking news can be the reason for fear. Some have expressed fear at the loss of business, when things have taken a downward spiral, at the sound of bad news. It could be a seed sown which has germinated and resulted in trouble for the person.

From a biblical point of view, we are told fear has torment and it has powers to bind people.

"Do not be afraid of their faces, for I am with you to deliver you," says the Lord." Jeremiah 1:8

"For God has not given us a spirit of fear, but of power and of love and of a sound mind." 2 Timothy 1:7

"Look! You are trusting in the staff of this broken reed, Egypt, on which if a man leans, it will go into his hand and pierce it. So is Pharaoh king of Egypt to all who trust in him. "But if you say to me, 'We trust in the Lord our God,' is it not He whose high places and whose altars Hezekiah has taken away, and said to Judah and Jerusalem, 'You shall worship before this altar'?"" Isaiah 36:6-7

"And Moses said to the people, "Do not be afraid. Stand still, and see the salvation of the Lord, which He will accomplish for you today. For the Egyptians whom you see today, you shall see again no more forever." Exodus 14:13

"You shall not be afraid of the terror by night, nor of the arrow that flies by day" Psalm 91:5

"When you go out to battle against your enemies, and see horses and chariots and people more numerous than you, do not be afraid of them; for the Lord your God is with you, who brought you up from the land of Egypt... And he shall say to them, 'Hear, O Israel: Today you are on the verge of battle with your enemies. Do not let your heart faint, do not be afraid, and do not tremble or be terrified because of them" Deuteronomy 20:1, 3

From the passages quoted, fear can come from words spoken, the expression on people's faces, the terror one can see or imagine and the size or number of people who have risen against you.

Fear is a blanket created by satan for his overt and covert operations. It is what can grip the heart of the believer and make him unable to witness or speak for Christ. It must be the reason why the Apostles prayed specifically for boldness to be able to preach the Word of Christ in the face of persecution.

"Now, Lord, look on their threats, and grant to Your servants that with all boldness they may speak Your word," Acts 4:29

THE CONSEQUENCES OF FEAR

Fear is a bad master. It can open up the doors to other issues.

> **Fear is a blanket created by satan for his overt and covert operations**

"A merry heart makes a cheerful countenance, but by sorrow of the heart the spirit is broken." Proverbs 15:13

"A merry heart does good, like medicine, but a broken spirit dries the bones." Proverbs 17:22

Fear is said to sometimes be a link between cancerous cells, heart trouble and other challenging sicknesses.

A fearful person can be put into bondage.

"The fear of man brings a snare, but whoever trusts in the Lord shall be safe." Proverbs 29:25

"For the thing I greatly feared has come upon me, and what I dreaded has happened to me." Job 3:25

Job was a righteous man who had trepidations and fears that things might go wrong. That particular phobia opened the door and gave the enemy a reason to be able to take advantage.

When a man walks in fear at its extreme, it can drain your joy, your victory. Fear also releases defeat, sadness and a sense of failure. That failure

Fear comes by hearing the word of the devil. Faith comes by hearing the Word of God

will lead to grumbling, complaining and a bitter spirit.

When a man is in this situation, his heart becomes a fertile ground for further phobias and stops them from being a good witness for Christ. Fear can stop the flow of faith and without faith you cannot please God.

Fear is a deadly and terrible enemy, a bad master. When you choose to yield to fear, you have chosen failure and frustrations. You have also opened doors to demonic infestations.

Fear is a faster destroyer than most other enemies. It raises false alarms and makes you say yes to untenable evidences. Fear is said in its acronym to mean "False Evidence Appearing Real."

It stops the flow of faith which would have released God into situations.

"Do not be afraid of them; the Lord your God himself will fight for you." Deuteronomy 3:22

Fear is a release mechanism, not for Christ but for satan. Fear and unbelief will keep you from moving into all that God has for you. It stops you from maximising your Christian life, your ministry, your relationship with God.

It makes you believe the carnal, satanic unbelieving report instead of the report of the Lord.

Fear and faith seem to be opposites. Fear comes by hearing the word of the devil. Faith comes by hearing the Word of God.

It magnifies your limitations, your financial challenges, your likely consequences compared to the godly confidences that can follow.

"Yet the Lord testified against Israel and against Judah, by all of His prophets, every seer, saying, "Turn from your evil ways, and keep My commandments and My statutes, according to all the law which I commanded your fathers, and which I sent to you by My servants the prophets."" 2 Kings 17:13

When a man goes through the midnights of life, fear takes advantage of that. It takes advantage of lonely hours and magnifies the battles you go through a thousand times.

"When you lie down, you will not be afraid; Yes, you will lie down and your sleep will be sweet. Do not be afraid of sudden terror, nor of trouble from the wicked when it

comes; for the Lord will be your confidence, and will keep your foot from being caught." Proverbs 3:24-26

Fear can bring death. People have been shocked and lost their mind and heart. When you fear, you become trapped.

"The fear of man brings a snare, but whoever trusts in the Lord shall be safe." Proverbs 29:25

The number one reason satan uses fear as a weapon is to destroy.

"The thief does not come except to steal, and to kill, and to destroy. I have come that they may have life, and that they may have it more abundantly." John 10:10

The Greek word for fear 'phobos' actually means to live in terror, to dread something, to anticipate or expect something bad to happen. It causes you to expect the worst. It can put you in danger of the very things you are afraid of.

Fear can make you shy and cause you to have a timid attitude to the point that you stop witnessing for Christ because you are afraid of being rejected, being criticised or being considered as a person imposing your own opinion.

Fear is capable of starting a battle you may not be able to handle. In the words of Alexis Carrol, 'fear is capable of starting a genuine disease'.

When you fear, you become trapped

Fear produces bondage and bondage is always the result of satan's work. When a little fear begins and is left unchecked, it becomes big fear. Big fear becomes a major bondage and the major bondage, if unchecked, becomes a doorway for the devil.

Fear has a way of binding people. We hear stories of people who are unable to leave their homes because a certain level of phobia has taken over their mind.

Fear will undermine your enthusiasm for living. It discourages initiatives and takes away the steps of faith, whereas without the steps of faith, there are several shores you will never discover.

Fear leads to uncertainty of purpose. It holds you back and encourages procrastination. Fear is the birthplace of mediocrity; that is activity without progress.

Fear kills love, and breeds jealousy and suspicion. Once you become afraid of people you should love, all kinds of assumptions come in. Assumptions lead to a lot of mess-ups.

> Only eternity will be able to adequately, accurately give the measure of some people's gifting who have been held back by a reversal gear of fear

Then there is the fear of rejection. Fear diverts your concentration and breaks your focus. It is a paralysing force that will severely handicap your potential to succeed. It builds invisible walls and erects barriers between people.

There is almost no war, civil or international, which does not have fear at its root. Racism is bred deeply by fear.

Fear can pull you away from serving God, saying "I am not good enough, I am not holy enough." Many have not prayed for the sick because they are afraid. A lot of middle-class Christians as we have deliberated on in this book have never witnessed for Christ for fear of rejection or being considered inferior.

Fear can make you an unfruitful and ineffective minister of the Gospel. How many gifted men have never really fully walked in the scope and dimension of their gift because they are afraid that if they take a step of faith, nothing supernatural may happen?

Fear can cause you to think and act irrationally and make stupid and panic-driven decisions. Fear is designed to hold you back and contain you so that it prevents you from going forward.

Only eternity will be able to adequately, accurately give the measure of some people's gifting who have been held back by a reversal gear of fear.

Fear can discourage a person and render them unable to sleep, which can lead to other health problems. Fear can destroy a person's capacity to rest and ultimately result in a loss of mind.

When I was a teenager, my father went on military guard. The tree in front of our house had cast a shadow on the window pane. In my young mind of a fourteen-year-old, I imagined it to be somebody standing behind our window. I screamed, "Who is there?" and nobody answered. I did not sleep until daybreak. Early in the morning I rushed out to see this person who would not leave, only to find out that it was a tree that had cast a shadow. I lost my sleep for the simple reason that fear had aggravated my imagination.

Fear can cause depression in your life and create terror. Terror involves dread and torment.

THE FEARLESS WALK

At the time of writing this book, a mindless gunman had walked into a mosque in New Zealand and gunned down 50 precious souls. That same week, close to 100 Christians were killed in Kaduna, Nigeria. The incident in Nigeria almost becoming a weekly occurrence, particularly in Kaduna State.

The death of these people in New Zealand received global attention, whereas the incident in Nigeria went unheeded. It is almost injurious to draw parallels and comparisons. All deaths are deaths. Lives are precious. But purely for the sake of illustration here, we need to draw the attention to the fact that middle class Nigerian Christians, a nation with an upsurge of Christian revival, has chosen to be numb and accept politically correct news about the death of people. One might only wonder, if it is for fear of reprisals, the possible burning of church buildings, or the killing of more Christians, that church leaders do not speak out.

The fearless walk means that you see yourself as

a fearless person. Fearless people explore the biology of fear. They know it was wired into them for protection, therefore, they are not afraid to be afraid when necessary, but

> **Fearless faith will require that we learn to speak out for the Gospel**

they use it as a way to stand and to overcome.

Always remember that much of it is in your mind and head. Be aware of your fear and overcome it. Rehearse the worst that can happen and put it behind you.

Fearless faith will require that we learn to speak out for the Gospel. Write action plans for dealing with fear. Many times, it will disappear when you do this.

Analyse what you could lose by permitting fear, but also imagine what you are losing by giving in to unnecessary fear. Fill your mind with who God wants you to be in the face of fear. Call up images of fearless role models and imitate them.

"Now all these things happened to them as examples, and they were written for our admonition, upon whom the ends of the ages have come." 1 Corinthians 10:11

Ensure that you realise that your tongue becomes a weapon for delivering you from every fear Take an interest in investigating what is the root of your fear. Objectivity might just destroy a lot of your anxiety.

Anoint your ears to hear the right thing. Refuse to be carried away by evil reports.

"He will not be afraid of evil tidings; his heart is steadfast, trusting in the Lord. His heart is established; he will not be afraid, until he sees his desire upon his enemies." Psalm 112:7-8

Be grateful for the privilege you have, and all kinds of fright will leave you. We say this in particular for those who have found themselves bound by fear when they have had to stand in front of people or express their faith.

Be grateful for the platform on which you stand to sing, speak, or share and the grip of fear will leave you.

Get someone who can both teach and encourage you to be a model in order to walk the fearless walk. That way, you will not be alone, and you will get the kind of feedback that will help you and not crush your spirit.

Before fear has its maximum impact, begin to gather all the scriptures that promise you victory. The Word of God is the sure instrument of victory in any situation.

So, refuse to act carnally by walking in worry, frustration, fear, confusion or other sinful attitudes. Look for the scriptures that promise you victory in particular situations and stand on them without thinking otherwise.

> *"He shall cover you with His feathers, and under His wings you shall take refuge; His truth shall be your shield and buckler." Psalm 91:4*

> *"A wholesome tongue is a tree of life, but perverseness in it breaks the spirit." Proverbs 15:4*

Ensure that you realise that your tongue becomes a weapon for delivering you from every fear. Let it be the weapon for speaking your victory. Let your tongue become that which makes your life a tree of life, the bridge of your spirit into good things. Let it become the protection of your life.

Speak with your mouth. Let the words of your mouth become a shield against negative attitudes and against what satan wants you to believe.

Visualise. Learn to see yourself doing the things you thought would kill you.

Speak the Word. Challenge people. Walk the fearless walk. Free yourself from being a control freak, where you are so afraid that you might get things wrong. Renounce every satanic deal that has been handed to you that does not belong to you.

Refuse to be fenced in. You are a free man in a free world so, develop an uncommon confidence which comes from the Holy Spirit. We dealt more about confidence in the previous chapter.

"For thus says the Lord God, the Holy One of Israel: "In returning and rest you shall be saved; in quietness and confidence shall be your strength." But you would not," Isaiah 30:15

"And Moses said to the people, "Do not be afraid. Stand still, and see the salvation of the Lord, which He will accomplish for you today. For the Egyptians whom you see today, you shall see again no more forever. The Lord will fight for you, and you shall hold your peace."" Exodus 14:13-14

The more confident you are the more fearless you become. Confidence will increase your security. Confidence will become even stronger when you get the facts on any matter and when you have the facts your fears are lessened.

The more experience you have in your chosen field the less fear grips you. So, the fearless walk requires that you grow in your faith, you grow in grace, and that you become a better person by stepping out.

You are a free man in a free world so, develop an uncommon confidence which comes from the Holy Spirit

Many people who fly once in a while dread flying but imagine the fact that this is the life of pilots. They too have families and their lives are precious, but they know something that the average flyer does not know; therefore, they are fearless.

Fearless people do not allow their confidence to be silenced. Fearless people prepare for eventualities. They make a plan. In fact, they over-prepare without over-reacting. No man is allowed to fly a plan without hours and hours of experience. That is preparing for eventualities. He sits in a simulator where he is made to go through the likely challenges that can occur.

Your actions determine your outcomes. Being fearless will make you know when to push forward or backward.

Choose a fearless walk, not a fearful stand

In a battle that is raging around believers today, Christians need to realise that they must remind themselves that above everything else, we have the joy of God.

"Then he said to them, "Go your way, eat the fat, drink the sweet, and send portions to those for whom nothing is prepared; for this day is holy to our Lord. Do not sorrow, for the joy of the Lord is your strength."" Nehemiah 8:10

"Therefore with joy you will draw water from the wells of salvation." Isaiah 12:3

"A merry heart does good, like medicine, but a broken spirit dries the bones." Proverbs 17:22

Confess the victories that you already hear in your spirit. Do not let fear overwhelm you. Always remember and recognise that fear is a fiery dart that satan shoots at people and he uses it to control.

Strengthen yourself!

"Strengthen the weak hands, and make firm the feeble knees. Say to those who are fearful-hearted, "Be strong, do not fear! Behold, your God will come with vengeance, with the recompense of God; He will come and save you."" Isaiah 35:3-4

"Then His disciples came to Him and awoke Him, saying,

"Lord, save us! We are perishing!" But He said to them, "Why are you fearful, O you of little faith?" Then He arose and rebuked the winds and the sea, and there was a great calm." Matthew 8:25-26

One of the most powerful things God has given you as a human being is the power to choose. So, choose a fearless walk, not a fearful stand.

"Do you not know that to whom you present yourselves slaves to obey, you are that one's slaves whom you obey, whether of sin leading to death, or of obedience leading to righteousness?" Romans 6:16

Remember, satan wants to condemn you and make you feel that you are not good enough, not pure enough, not passionate enough, whereas God sees your heart and He will deliver you from fear.

"I sought the Lord, and He heard me, and delivered me from all my fears." Psalm 34:4

"For He satisfies the longing soul, and fills the hungry soul with goodness." Psalm 107:9

"Do not fear, nor be afraid; have I not told you from that time, and declared it? You are My witnesses. Is there a God besides Me? Indeed there is no other Rock; I know not one.'" Isaiah 44:8

Tear down every stronghold the enemy wants to build around your life in your walk.

"casting down arguments and every high thing that exalts itself against the knowledge of God, bringing every thought into captivity to the obedience of Christ,"
2 Corinthians 10:5

Every time satan shoots a contrary thought, defy it with the Word of God. Every time he tells you to be a man of fear, remind him that your Leader's nature is that of love, joy, peace and long-suffering.

"For the kingdom of God is not eating and drinking, but righteousness and peace and joy in the Holy Spirit."
Romans 14:17

When you do not know what to do, part of your fearless walk is to stand still and see what God will do.

"And Moses said to the people, "Do not be afraid. Stand still, and see the salvation of the Lord, which He will accomplish for you today. For the Egyptians whom you see today, you shall see again no more forever."
Exodus 14:13

---

[6] https://en.wikipedia.org/wiki/Fear

Fearless Faith

CONCLUSION

You are called to walk in Fearless Faith This book has been concluded during the biggest pandemic that has hit the planet in modern times; the Coronavirus. It has sent jitters down the spine of presidents and injected fears into all parts of society.

Permit me to say that satan has ridden on the back of a virus and spread fear like wild fire.

Fear is satan's source of power, that is why he likes to fan it continually. Major playgrounds arounds the world are absolutely empty; the Eiffel Tower, Times Square, New York, the Arc de Triomphe, the gondolas of Venice, restaurants and theatres. Fear makes it look like planet earth has a taken a break.

The finished work of Christ on the cross of Calvary establishes the truth that we are bravehearts. We are a people called to be more than conquerors. We are the champions league, a force of confidence, the company of the fearless.

It is time to lift up your head and affirm every day who you are in Christ. Reach forth, take responsibility for your life.

Your daily affirmations must include the fact that:

- You are a joint heir with Christ
- You refuse to have a fearful heart
- You have abundance spiritually, physically and financially
- You are a child of the king
- You are called to reign

MATTHEW ASHIMOLOWO MEDIA MINISTRIES

www.pastormatthew.tv	www.amazon.com
iTunes store	**Kindle store**

Ghana Motivational Media Limited: P.O. Box AN 19792

Accra-North

Tel: +233 243 69 00 71

Nigeria 13 Oki Lane, Mende,

Maryland,

Lagos, Nigeria.

Tel: + 234 1 899 8822/8833

United Kingdom KICC Prayer City

Buckmore Park

Chatham, Kent ME5 9QG

Tel: +44(0)845 130 3471

USA Matthew Ashimolowo Ministries, P.O. Box 470470,

Tulsa, OK 74147-0470.

Tel: +1-800 717 0571

Contact Matthew Ashimolowo

Twitter   @MatAshimolowo

Instagram   ma.ashimolowo

Facebook   Matthew A. Ashimolowo